Divided by Gender, United by Chocolate: Differences in the Boardroom

Dr Fiona Beddoes-Jones

D1354734

Blue Ocean Publishing

Divided by Gender, United by Chocolate: Differences in the Boardroom

© Fiona Beddoes-Jones, PhD, 2016

Published by Blue Ocean Publishing
St John's Innovation Centre
Cambridge CB4 0WS
United Kingdom

http://www.blueoceanpublishing.biz

A catalogue record for this book is available from the British Library.

ISBN 978-1-907527-28-9

First published in the United Kingdom in 2016 by Blue Ocean Publishing.

For Mark, and those like him, who risk their lives
so the rest of us can live in peace,
and pursue our dreams.

This book is dedicated to the brave men and women of
Her Majesty's Coastguard in the UK, with whom I had the
honour and privilege to work in 2014 and 2015.

Acknowledgements

The first person I want to thank is Dr Helen Fisher, the brilliant American anthropologist who originally identified the four hormonally-driven temperament types around which this book is based. It was her book on dating and relationships, *Why Him, Why Her?* which first alerted me to how our biological, hormonal make-up could affect our thinking and behaviours. As I was doing my doctoral research into Authentic Leadership at the time, it seemed only natural that I should take her research and apply it to the area of leadership style to formulate my own theory of Leadership Temperament Types.

The second people I would like to thank are my parents; all of them. Like many people in our modern world, due to divorce and remarriage I have more than one set. They have made me who I am today, and whilst they readily admit that they don't always understand the work I do, they are, and have always been, unswervingly supportive, something for which I am always thankful.

Many friends and colleagues have kindly contributed to the book by completing the various questionnaires within it and then discussing their results with me so I could be sure that my ideas and theories actually worked in practice. You will be pleased to know that they do! Some of these generous people agreed to be case studies for the book. You will find their stories, and their scores, in Chapter 9.

My grateful thanks to you all.

Contents

About the Author

I have often wondered about choices. When an option is in front of us, tempting us to choose a future direction like three possibilities at a crossroads, the choice we take may lead us on to a future that we didn't for one moment imagine.

When, at 27, I embarked on a personal development course in London, using up my annual holiday from what is now Celerant/Hitachi Consulting to do so, I did not envisage that it would nudge me quite so strongly towards where I have ended up: as a Chartered Psychologist with a PhD in Authentic Leadership and my own international consulting company working with great people in clients such as BP, Airbus, Coutts Bank, Her Majesty's Coastguard and the UK military services.

As the author of the psychometric tools Thinking Styles™, Cognitive Team Roles™, Think Smart™ and the Authentic Leadership 360™, I specialise in linking thinking to behaviour; in helping people to understand more about themselves and other people, increasing their self-awareness and, I hope, improving the quality of all their relationships, including the critical relationship that they have with themselves.

It is with that at the forefront of my mind that I offer you this book, in the hope that the thoughts and suggestions which you find contained within it will somehow help you too in understanding your personal and professional relationships, and in improving them.

My very best wishes,

Fiona Beddoes-Jones

Background

In the spring of 2013, I received a phone call from Bournemouth University in the UK. Through the military grapevine they had heard about the work I had done with the UK's Royal Air Force on Authentic Leadership, and we had a great conversation around different leadership styles and how men and women, in general, may lead differently to each other, whilst still being authentic leaders in their own ways.

As a result of our telephone discussion around leadership, the university subsequently invited me to deliver the inaugural lecture for their Women's Academic Network in September 2013. Germaine Greer wasn't available apparently, although she subsequently addressed them in a packed house in June 2014. Naturally, I was honoured to be asked in her absence, and with Authentic Leadership being the most obvious choice, as that is the subject of my PhD research, I spent quite some time thinking about what exactly I could talk about that would interest and amuse the audience, which was to be a mixture of both men and women.

In the end I did speak about Authentic Leadership and my doctoral research into it. However, I also spoke about something else; I talked about the brilliant work that the American anthropologist Dr Helen Fisher has done on what she calls *Temperament Types*, and I applied it, for the first time, to leadership. In addition, I also spoke about the equally brilliant work which Professor Simon Baron-Cohen from Cambridge University in the UK has done regarding the exploration and understanding of the autistic spectrum and what he calls the *Extreme Male Brain*, and I also applied that to leadership and leadership style preference.

I called my lecture *Divided by Gender, United by Chocolate: Differences in the Boardroom.*

It was so well received, and so many people came up to me afterwards and asked if I had written a questionnaire that they could complete to identify their own Leadership Temperament Type preferences, or a book about it all that they could read, I decided that perhaps I should write one! Three years later, the book you are now reading is that book.

So I would like to thank Bournemouth University for having the faith in me to ask me to support their new Women's Academic Network, which has subsequently gone from strength to strength. I would also like to thank once again all of those friends and colleagues who supported me in my thinking regarding my theories and research for this book, especially those who generously gave up their time to test the questionnaires which are included within it, and which you can also find at *www.unitedbychocolate.com*.

Before we begin to explore what this book is all about and the theories and ideas it contains, I would like to invite you to consider the following questions:

1. Do you want to succeed at work?

2. Have you ever wondered why some people seem to be natural leaders whilst other people seem to struggle with the role?

3. Do you aspire to a leadership or management role?

4. Would you like to understand more about leadership and management styles and know what yours might be?

5. How do you feel about your boss? Do you aspire to be like them or do you think that you could do a better job, given the chance?

6. Have you ever been bullied at work or seen someone bully others?

7. Would you be interested in learning how to influence your colleagues or your boss?

8. Do you have an interest in building long-term and sustainable effective working relationships?

9. Do you think that men and women tend to lead in different ways?

10. Is winning important to you?

The more times you have answered yes to any of these questions, the more interesting, insightful and beneficial you will find this book to be. Together, we are going to unravel and explore this new theory of leadership. I believe it underpins and explains leadership through the ages and the gendered leadership imbalance that is prevalent in leadership and leadership stereotypes today, on a global level. By this I mean that today, stereotypically, when we think about leadership and leaders, particularly senior and powerful leaders, we automatically think that these leaders will be male. There's more on gendered leadership and leadership style stereotypes in Chapters 1 and 2.

Because they are easier to find and work with, it's very often the case in the UK that students are used for doctoral and post-doctoral academic research. I was absolutely adamant however that I wouldn't do that with my PhD research. Rather than involving students with no real-world leadership experience, I was determined to do my research using real leaders, making my research into Authentic Leadership both more relevant and arguably, more accurate, than research undertaken either in the artificial environment of the laboratory or in the artificial context of using students. After presenting my research ideas at the 2007 International Studying Leadership Conference in the UK, I was fortunate to be invited to work with the UK military, with senior serving Royal Air Force officers.

We are going to be considering Authentic Leadership; what it is and what it means for you. Within the West, the concepts of authenticity and being authentic have become very popular over the past decade. However, there is a big difference between being authentic, (small a, used as an adjective), as a person and as a leader or manager, and being an *Authentic Leader*, (capital A, capital L, used as a noun). My

PhD research identified that there are some specific criteria for being able to be described as an Authentic Leader, and I am delighted to be able to share these with you. An interesting theory regarding leadership failure and the three fundamental reasons why a leader, any leader, will fail also emerged from my research and I will also share this with you.

In Chapter 1, we are going to begin by exploring some interesting findings that you may not be aware of about gender stereotyping. As a starting point, to support our thinking about male and female gender stereotypes we will be considering the people/task continuum and what that might mean for your, and other people's, preferences regarding their leadership and management style approaches. We will be building on that by looking at Professor Simon Baron-Cohen's theory regarding the Extreme Male Brain and its links to the autistic spectrum of behaviours.

Chapter 2 explores and discusses the current gender divide in the Boardroom, and considers gendered leadership stereotyping. It highlights some of the things that are being done to address the gender imbalance in organisations, especially at the highest levels. I explain how addressing the gender divide in the Boardroom by considering such things as women-only shortlists is an error of thinking brought about by a failure to understand what's really going on. The current approach to diversity from the perspective of the gender balance/imbalance in the boardroom is a red herring which seems to have fooled everyone, possibly because, up until now, there hasn't been another viable theory to explain gendered leadership and its implications for leadership style preference at senior executive and board levels.

The theory of Dr Helen Fisher's four biologically-driven Temperament Types are introduced and described in Chapter 3. They are the dopamine-driven Explorer; the oestrogen-driven Negotiator; the testosterone-driven Director and the serotonin-driven Builder. They relate to Charismatic, Relational, Transactional, and Transformational leadership styles respectively. This is your opportunity to begin to think about which Leadership Temperament Type or types might be your natural preferences and therefore what the implications of that are for you at work, and possibly at home too.

Chapter 4 is the science bit. Here we review some of the supporting research and evidence which underpins the theory of Leadership Temperament Types and we look specifically at how the hormone or neurotransmitter associated with each type might affect our behaviours at work, especially in a leadership role.

Which type are you? This is the question that we answer in Chapter 5, where you will find the main diagnostics of the book. Here, you can identify your primary and secondary preferences from amongst the four Leadership Temperament Types. In fact, you can identify your percentage scores for all of the four Leadership Temperament Types. Chapter 5 is supported by *www.unitedbychocolate.com* where you will find some other diagnostic questionnaires, optional reports and also links to more information and further resources, including a link to the best chocolate I have ever tasted!

By the time you get to the next chapter you will probably be wondering about the potential weaknesses and downsides of each Leadership Temperament Type. After all, poor behaviours can derail someone's career, including yours, so it is useful to be able to recognise where they come from and understand them. So leading, managing and influencing are the topics we explore and discuss in Chapter 6, as well as how the Leadership Temperament Types interact in practical terms.

The Dark Side of Leadership has fascinated me ever since I read *Snakes in Suits* a few years go and recognised some of the people I had been working with for years! In Chapter 7 I lift the lid on some research you might not have come across before regarding management and leadership failure and we consider which of the four

Leadership Temperament Types are most likely to exhibit derailing leadership behaviours or suffer from *Hubris Syndrome.*

As I've already mentioned, Authentic Leadership was the area of my original doctoral research. A great deal has been written about the subject, both academically and from a practitioner perspective, and in Chapter 8 we will untangle some of its knots so that by unravelling it we can see it and understand it more clearly. Being authentic as a person, especially if you have a leadership role, is not the same as being an Authentic Leader.   History tells us that much with every story of every dictator who has ever lived. So here I explain the difference between being *authentic* and *Authentic Leadership*. I will also share with you The 3 Reasons Why Leaders Fail.

Chapter 9 explores Authentic Leadership *in action*. Whilst being authentic in their own ways, Charismatic, Relational, Transactional and Transformational leaders will all lead differently, as each Leadership Temperament Type is underpinned by a different biological driver and is therefore motivated by different things. This chapter includes ten case studies of real leaders who have generously shared their profiles and actual scores with us to illustrate how the four Leadership Temperament Types can combine to operate in practice.

The theory of Leadership Temperament Types is such a game changer that we won't ever be able to think about leadership, especially gendered leadership or leadership in the Boardroom, in the ways that we used to, ever again. Therefore The Future of the Boardroom takes centre stage in Chapter 10. This chapter ties all the threads of the theory together and also includes a 5-Point Plan for ensuring Board success with some suggestions for developing Authentic Leadership at both individual and organisational levels.

In the Epilogue, I share with you my hopes for the future regarding the Leadership Temperament Types model, and what I believe it can potentially achieve on the global corporate stage.

Chapter 1: Gender Stereotypes

Stereotyping is a way of combining together the attributes of a group of people or things into a shared social concept that we all understand. A stereotype is therefore a *heuristic*; a kind of useful cognitive shortcut to stop us from having to think too hard about the characteristics of the people who make up the group. *'Pink for a girl and blue for a boy'* is a typical modern, culturally derived, western gender stereotype with which we are all familiar, although interestingly, historically, the colours were reversed. It was only in the 1950's and 60's that pink became more associated with femininity. As heuristics, stereotypes and stereotyping can be useful to us, apart from the fact that stereotypes are rarely the actual reality, because of course there are always exceptions to every rule of thumb. Whilst we all use them, we should also be aware that they are going to be wrong at times and so we should use them mindfully and with caution.

Interestingly, we all intuitively know that the whole gender stereotyping thing doesn't really work anyway. Whilst the Conservatives were elected on economic policy and an effective electoral campaign in 1979, when Margaret Thatcher became the first female Prime Minister of the United Kingdom many UK residents thought that it might herald a new era of politics and culture; an era of gentler, less aggressive and less combative politics, with a greater focus on collaboration and nurturing perhaps. Margaret Thatcher was a mother after all. How mistaken and naïve we were! Margaret Thatcher, it turned out, was more dominant, aggressive and competitive than the vast majority of male politicians, in both her own Conservative cabinet and those of the Liberal and Labour opposition parties.

Just because Margaret Thatcher was a woman, is there any reason why we should think that she would be kind, gentle and nurturing? Actually, research suggests that that's exactly what we would think[1]. Stereotypically, we expect women to be collaborative and compliant, both at work and at home. We somehow expect them to be kind, loving, gentle, supportive, understanding, communicative, empathetic, intuitive, altruistic and compassionate. However, whilst some men are indeed like this, clearly not all women are.

Moreover, when a woman goes against female stereotypical expectations and behaves in ways which are not considered naturally feminine and nurturing, but which are more 'masculine', research also suggests that she is judged much more harshly for her actions than we would judge a man for doing the same thing[1]. We seem to have certain assumptions regarding men and women in management and leadership roles which, in practice, do not always turn out to be correct. While not going into the whole gendered leadership styles debate, (there are other books around for that), this book will give you a new perspective towards understanding some of the reasons why people behave as they do. It will also provide insights into leader and manager behaviours, and it will even explore people's neuro-biological motivations for achieving such positions of responsibility in the first place. First and foremost however, and perhaps this is the most important thing of all, this book will help you to understand *yourself*.

As a UK Chartered Psychologist who is focused on linking thinking and behaviour, I've always maintained that *the thinking comes first*. Sometimes it's deliberate, but even if the thinking is either unconscious, or is an emotional response, there is definitely something that happens within us before our actual behaviour occurs. We rationalise it by calling it either intuition or strategy. I used to believe, probably somewhat arrogantly in retrospect, that I had somehow managed to get it right by tracking back from the behaviour to the underpinning thinking which motivated it. It was this line of thought which led me to develop the Thinking Styles™ questionnaire and report to assist people in understanding their own cognitive style strategies and enabling them to think more effectively. Nearly twenty years later I now realise that I was only right up to a point. I have now come to the belief that in part, it is our biological/hormonal make-up which influences and drives our thinking and therefore our subsequent behaviours. I had missed a step and not tracked things back far enough!

I'm now going to introduce you to a model that you may already be familiar with. Whether you are aware of it or not, it forms the basis of a number of modern theories around leadership and leadership approaches. It has been recognised that there are significant differences in the way that leaders, (and in fact everybody, not just leaders), consider these two things as far back as the ancient Greeks and Romans. It is the People/Task Continuum.

People vs Task Focus

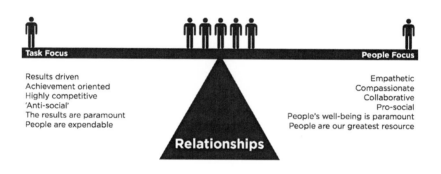

© Fiona Beddoes-Jones 2015   www.unitedbychocolate.com   www.cognitivefitness.co.uk

I have simplified the model for you and summarised the key principles. As you can see, the continuum is effectively a model of opposites and I've put these opposite beliefs and behaviours at each end of the scale. The people on the continuum represent the distribution curve. As with all normal distribution curves, where the sample size is large enough, there will be more people whose preference is in the middle of the scale than there will be at each end of it, as statistically speaking, 68% of people will always fall within the 'average' range. The triangle upon which the continuum balances contains the word 'relationships'. This is because relationships underpin the model; where you sit on the scale will effect and affect the relationships that you have with your colleagues.

To explain the model I am going to describe the beliefs and behaviours at the extreme ends of the scale. Most people, while they will have tendencies in a particular direction, will not think or behave quite so radically. People with a Task Focus are very achievement oriented, they are highly competitive, often believing that the end justifies the means and they will cut corners, even being unethical in their decisions and behaviours, so strong is their desire to win. For them, the results they want to achieve are paramount, and for them, people are expendable. At the extreme end of the Task Focused scale we are likely to see a small percentage of people exhibiting 'leadership detailers'. We will be exploring these in more depth in Chapter 7.

In contrast, those leaders and managers with a People Focus are very others oriented, and are highly pro-social, being focused on developing long-term, positive, sustainable relationships. For them, people are the most important consideration, above the task and the results. They are kind, caring, very supportive of colleagues and highly collaborative. They strongly believe that all tasks, objectives, outcomes and results are ultimately for the benefit of people, and they are much more interested in, and driven by, compassion and empathy than they are by either winning or achieving set objectives and corporate results. They don't derail as such, but rather, without any focus on goals, targets, objectives and outputs, they are much less likely to be promoted to positions of leadership in the first instance.

Do you know where your preference is on the scale? Do you have one set point on the scale or do you have the behavioural and cognitive flexibility to move up and down it? Here are two exercises that I have used in management and leadership development programmes across all industries and sectors for many years and they are always a source of interest and debate.

Exercise 1

- Put an 'X' on the scale that is your normal set point at work. This is your *position 1*.

- Put a second 'X' on the scale where you are when you are being your absolute best self. This is your *position 2*.

- What do you already notice about the difference in position between the two 'X' points? How is the quality of your relationships with other people affected here, when you are being your best self? How is the quality of your relationship with yourself affected? What insights does this simple exercise give you already?

- Where does your 'X' move to when you are under stress and pressure at work? This is your *position 3*.

- How are your relationships with your team, your colleagues, your boss and your family and friends affected when you are in position 3? What things might you be able to do so that you can get back into your position 1, and ideally, your best-self position 2? There will be actions and strategies that you can put in place which will support you. And, in fact, the best time to do them will be as soon as you notice yourself beginning to move from your position 1.

I can guarantee at least two things here: firstly, that your position 3 X won't be in the same place as it is at position 2 when you are being your best self; and secondly, that when you are under stress in position 3, the quality of your relationships with those around you and probably with yourself will be affected, and not in a good way. If you want to print out a copy of the model so you can physically plot your various positions on the continuum, you can download it free of charge at *www.unitedbychocolate.com*.

Exercise 2

- This exercise will identify your range of flexibility on the continuum. Looking at Diagram 1, put an 'A' on the left side where you feel comfortable operating up to, bearing in mind that your task focus will become more extreme, (at the expense of people), the further towards the left end of the scale you go.

- Now put a 'B' on the right side of the continuum towards the People Focus end of the scale where you also feel comfortable operating.

- Join the two points, 'A' and 'B' with a straight line, putting a little arrow head for clarity, like this, <-------> . This represents your 'comfort zone' on the continuum.

- Now add two more arrows, also with double arrow heads, on the other side of your 'A' and 'B' points, like this <----> A< -----> B <-------> (remember your arrows will be the length that is representative of your scores and may not look like the ones I have used here for illustrating the point). These two new outside arrows represent your ability to operate on the scale outside of your comfort zone.

- This is very useful information to have, especially when you can recognise it. In fact, the military in the UK design many of their leadership development exercises deliberately to push people outside of their natural area of comfort whilst still being able to operate effectively, until such a time when they can move back to within their comfort zone. This is especially critical in a war zone situation where a leader's order may well mean that, potentially, not all of their military personnel may come back in one piece, or at all.

- The longer your lines are and the more of the continuum you are able to cover, the greater your flexibility will be, and therefore the more flexible, supportive and yet achievement-oriented you will be.

Let's see whether there's any scientific evidence to support the People/Task Continuum theory and at the same time let's also consider what else might potentially be going on in the bodies and brains of men and women from a biological perspective.

I would like to introduce you to the work of Simon Baron-Cohen, Professor of Developmental Psychopathology at the University of Cambridge in the UK. He is the Director of the University's Autism Research Centre, and has spent more than 20 years working with people who have autism. He has developed a theory which he calls *Extreme Male Brain Theory*[2]. Whilst the majority of people diagnosed on the autistic spectrum are male, according to recent research, there is a significant percentage of women who also have autism and therefore paradoxically also seem to have predominantly *male* brains! Could this also mean then that potentially there is a significant percentage of men who could be said to have predominantly *female* brains?

I've adapted Baron-Cohen's theory for you in Diagram 2 so that it's easier to understand some of the differences between a 'male' and a 'female' brain. Of course, there's no such thing as a gendered brain *per se*; however, as a framework and as a psychological metaphor, viewing the brain through the lens of behaviours which are predominantly male compared to behaviours which are predominantly female, does seem to yield a useful perspective.

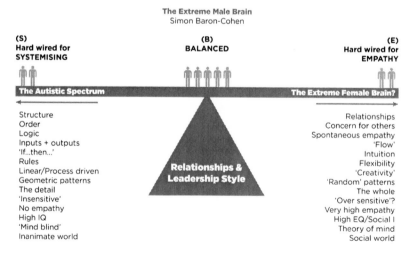

The Extreme Male Brain
Simon Baron-Cohen

(S) Hard wired for SYSTEMISING	(B) BALANCED	(E) Hard wired for EMPATHY
The Autistic Spectrum		The Extreme Female Brain?
Structure	Relationships &	Relationships
Order	Leadership Style	Concern for others
Logic		Spontaneous empathy
Inputs + outputs		'Flow'
'If...then...'		Intuition
Rules		Flexibility
Linear/Process driven		'Creativity'
Geometric patterns		'Random' patterns
The detail		The whole
'Insensitive'		'Over sensitive'?
No empathy		Very high empathy
High IQ		High EQ/Social I
'Mind blind'		Theory of mind
Inanimate world		Social world

Adapted from Baron-Cohen, S., (2002). The extreme male brain theory of autism. *Trends in Cognitive Sciences*, Vol. 6, (6) pp.248–254.

Diagram 2 details a number of different and, similar to the earlier People/Task continuum, seemingly opposite behaviours and ways of thinking. At one end of the scale we have the extreme male brain, which Baron-Cohen suggests is 'hard-wired' for Systemising things, and at the other end of the scale we have the extreme female brain, which is hard-wired for Empathising with others. Hard-wiring is a concept which suggests a biological pre-disposition within the brain for thinking in a certain way. This is compared to neurological, 'brain plasticity' which is a concept suggesting the flexibility of the brain to lay down new neural pathways for thinking and behaving.

The Autistic Spectrum exists at the extreme male brain side of the scale, with autistic behaviours increasing in predominance and severity the further away from the middle of the scale you go. At the opposite end of the scale there is the extreme female brain, and according to some recent research, at this end of the scale there is a percentage of people who display psychosis, i.e. a distorted sense of reality, and that more of them are female than male[3]. In the middle section of the scale there is a balance of male and female behaviours, suggesting the behavioural flexibility to engage usefully in both male and female cognitive and behavioural strategies.

I would suggest that we don't exist at one point of the scale, but rather like the People/Task Continuum, we have an x and y point of behaviours within which we feel comfortable operating. In other words, we have a spectrum of behaviours and strategies, and it is very likely that there will be some similarities for you in your scores and ranges for each of the two models. For some people, their comfort range might be quite short, whilst others will have a much broader range. Additionally, people's ranges might start and end at different points. Once again, the longer someone's span is on the scale, the more flexible their cognitive, emotional and behavioural strategies will be. Therefore the more adaptable and effective team member, colleague and leader they will be.

If you would like to download the diagram and plot your own range, you will find it on the book's website at *www.unitedbychocolate.com* where you can download it free of charge.

Baron-Cohen suggests that the autistic, male brain is hard-wired for systemising. The Systemising brain is highly logical with structure and order being extremely important to the person. They are very uncomfortable with ambiguity as they need everything to be clearly defined and precise. I've used the word need here deliberately. Towards the middle of the scale, in the balanced region, someone may prefer, want or desire structure and order, logic, precision and definition. The nearer towards the extreme end of the male brain scale someone operates at, the more they actually have a cognitive, emotional and possibly even physical need for these things.

Because the Systemising brain is so linear, it functions on rules, often ones it makes up itself, (if they seem logical to it). It also operates on *'if, … then'* rules and with a focus on the inputs and outputs of a system or of the elements within the system, be that mathematics, physics or counting Lego bricks. The Systemising brain likes straight lines and geometric patterns, and, consistent with precision, definition, focused attention and logic, craves detail.

The focus on systemising, compared to a focus on empathising with other people, means that at the extreme, people who have this kind of cognitive and emotional preference can be perceived as being insensitive and lacking empathy. Whilst they may sometimes have a high intelligence quotient, (IQ, with its focus on logic), they may well be 'mind blind'. This is a psychological term which suggests that they are not able to formulate a Theory of Mind regarding what other people might be thinking or feeling. Normally developed pre-school children of about three years of age can predict that if a sibling or friend loses a much cherished toy, they will feel sad and may even cry about it. A child, manager or leader who is mind blind is incapable of understanding someone else's perspective or empathising with them, and will appear very cold and uncaring. They feel much more at home within an inanimate world of numbers, things or avatars on a computer, than they do with real people.

Real people however are very much the focus of the person with an Empathising brain, a brain Baron-Cohen calls an 'extreme female brain'. It's no accident that when we teasingly accuse a man of being in touch with his feminine side, we are effectively recognising their compassionate, caring, kind and nurturing people-oriented behaviours. The Empathising brain is hard-wired to focus on other people and relationships and to read faces in ways a mind-blind person is simply not able to. This results in an empathising person having a very high emotional intelligence quotient, and equally high social intelligence. It is the social world which fascinates them and is the focus of their attention. At this end of this scale someone would be highly intuitive and would also be flexible in the sense that they are comfortable with spontaneity and ambiguity.

You will see that I have said 'creativity?' regarding the Empathising brain. This is because here, people are 'creative' by connecting seemingly random thoughts and events, which of course don't seem random to them, but would seem so to a more logical and linear thinker. The question mark is used because it's perfectly possible to be creative logically as well. However, when we think of creativity, we usually think of it as it manifests itself at this end of the scale, with an intuitive, spontaneous, innovative, imaginative and original approach.

I have also used the word 'flow'. I've used it to describe a brain which becomes completely absorbed in something in the moment. In psychology, a 'flow experience' is one where we are completely immersed in a task with a feeling of enjoyment and energised focus. It's the state that we go into when we meditate or when we become completely absorbed by our favourite hobby. Time seems to stand still, and yet the time we spend also seems to pass in an instant. In sports we often refer to it as being 'in the zone'. I would suggest that it's the Empathising brain which moves into this state most readily and easily, as the Systemising brain becomes focused rather than relaxed when something engages its attention.

After many years of studying people's thinking and behaviours, I have come to believe that there is genius at both ends of the continuum. Probably not right at the very ends, possibly there we do indeed find autism and psychosis as Baron-Cohen and his colleagues suggest. However, I do think that perhaps we may find it a little way in from the very ends of the scale in people who are flexible enough to also be able to access and use the benefits that the opposite end of the scale offers; in other words, people who can be both highly logical and highly intuitive.

Have you recognised the similarities between the two models of the People/Task Focus continuum and the Extreme Male/Female Brain? According to our cultural gender stereotypes, women are expected to be generally more selfless, nurturing and concerned with others than men; this is known as being more communal. In contrast, men are expected to be, and are generally perceived as being, more agentic, that is, more assertive and motivated to master and control others[4].

This book is called *Divided by Gender*, and there is no doubt that there are indeed physical biological differences between the two sexes; even five-year-old children understand that. However, having biological sex differences regarding genitalia, doesn't mean that all men will be agentic and all women will be communal, as we all know from our own experience. As both models show quite clearly, just because someone has a certain physical gender, it doesn't mean that we can accurately predict how they will think or behave when it comes to decision-making. Gender diversity is an illusion from that perspective. Gender doesn't help us in predicting how someone will approach an ethical dilemma or even, more generally, their working style and their manner towards their colleagues.

We need diversity of thinking not diversity of gender;
it's not a sex thing!

This book and the theory of Leadership Temperament Types will forever change the way that we think about diversity in the Boardroom, which is what we are now going on to explore in Chapter 2 where we are going to learn more about gendered leadership and leadership stereotypes.   Let's see if they stand up to scrutiny any better than gender diversity has regarding men and women's stereotypical thinking and behaviour.

Chapter 2: Women-only Shortlists Don't Work

In the previous chapter, we explored the major gender stereotype that we have regarding how we expect men and women to behave. Stereotypes can be a useful heuristic; that is, a rule of thumb or mental shortcut to our thinking which helps us to manage our lives and make our daily decisions without having to expend too much cognitive effort. Heuristics regarding gender are particularly useful because they allow us to make certain assumptions about the kind of thinking and actions we expect people to take. This is most likely to be a social evolutionary device designed for survival; for example, males with higher baseline levels of testosterone tend to have broader brows, broader shoulders and more muscle mass. They are also likely to be more aggressive. A stranger exhibiting these physical qualities would therefore potentially have been more of a threat and more dangerous. So, heuristics can be useful, particularly gender ones.

The problem with heuristics and stereotyping is that once we have one, we then unconsciously look for confirmation of our expectations. Psychologists call it 'confirmation bias'. This is why we expect women, particularly mothers, to be nurturing and kind, gentle and considerate. Because the majority of women, especially mothers, are indeed this way, it is an enormous shock to the collective social psyche when they are not[1]. The same is true of men. Stereotypically, we expect them to be decisive, charismatic, dominant, aggressive if threatened or needing to protect their family, and competitive. Of course, we all know both men and women who fit these stereotypical portrayals of the genders. However, we also all know people who *don't* fit them.

Why do we need women-only shortlists in the first place?

The short answer is because it's not a level playing field and the world isn't fair! The reason it's not a level playing field or a fair one is because of things like gender stereotyping, confirmation bias, the think manager, think male paradigm, stereotype threat, the lack of fit leadership model, the glass cliff and the glass escalator. And that's before we add testosterone, status threat and hostile stereotyping into the mix! Add to this some statistical data on the actual position in the UK and the reason why women-only shortlists were brought in becomes clearer.

We know that diversity is a good thing. It encourages broader perspectives, increases creativity, innovation and effective problem-solving, positively impacts on well-being and makes groups more productive. This is true of all teams and groups by the way, not just senior leadership ones. Power and status appear to be of universal interest, therefore the gender balance within the Boardroom also continues to be of interest globally to organisations, politicians, the media and the public, and we now have international targets for female leadership representation[2]. The UK Davies Report[3], commissioned in 2010 to research the gender imbalance in UK FTSE Boards and published in 2011, recommended a target of 25% female representation on all UK FTSE 100 organisations by 2015.

By January 2015, the target figure had not been achieved. However, the Women on Boards Davies Review, a Five Year Summary[4], published in October 2015, details two landmark results: firstly, the percentage figure of women on FTSE 100 Boards has now reached 26.1%. Secondly, there are now no all-male Boards in any of the FTSE 100 companies. There are still 15 all-male Boards within the FTSE 250 companies where female representation stands at only 19.6% however, and the new report calls for 33% female representation within all FTSE 350 companies by 2020.

Outside the Boardroom, according to the 2015 Cranfield Female FTSE Board Report, despite progress being made on FTSE 100 companies, in 2015, only 8.6% of UK Executive Directorships were held by women[5]. That's a staggering 91.4% of them being held by men.

Why is there such a huge division of male and female leadership at this level? There are a number of different theories. At one end of the spectrum there is the suggestion that, as women still bear the majority of caring responsibility in the home for children, managing the household and ageing parents, they simply don't want the added stress of a senior position as well. At the other end of the spectrum is the suggestion that women are simply unsuited to senior leadership positions as they are somehow inferior to men at that level, although, thankfully, we have moved beyond the Victorian assertion that this is because women's brains are smaller than their masculine counterparts![6]

As much as you may either laugh or gasp in horror at this outrageous and blatantly ridiculous statement, there is a growing body of research to suggest that, regarding gender and leadership stereotyping, many people do indeed think that way, even if their bias is unconscious[7].

Gendered leadership

Are all leader stereotypes masculine? The answer to that, very simply, is that yes, they are![8] Historically, because men have traditionally occupied the leadership roles in the military, the church and in politics, their generally agentic leadership style has become the benchmark that has come to define leadership. It has also therefore become the standard by which leadership, and all the managers and leaders who practise it, both male and female, are judged[9]. This explains the 'think manager, think male' paradigm. Even today, in studies of implicit association, women are more associated with the liberal arts, domesticity, family, low status and low authority roles, whereas men are associated with science and maths, high status, high authority, hierarchy and careers[10]. Effectively, there is a 'lack of fit' between women and leadership that we are not consciously aware of. If you pay some attention to media advertising, particularly on the television, you will see these gendered leadership roles played out in the stereotypical roles which even quite young children pick up on and absorb culturally as the way things are. But more on that later.

The discussions around gendered leadership centre on two key themes: firstly, do men and women lead similarly or differently? And therefore, secondly, which gender tends to lead 'better' than the other?

Some studies indicate that women, consistent with the female leadership stereotype, do indeed tend to adopt more relational, participative and communal styles, characterised by a selfless, nurturing, caring approach with the well-being and welfare of others at its core. In comparison, men are more likely to take a more transactional, directive style, and be more agentic. This approach is characterised by a task/goal orientation, assertiveness, control, social domination and a desire to master[11]. This is consistent with the gender stereotyping which we encountered in Chapter 1 and the Empathising/Systemising theory of Baron-Cohen. Remember though, that the important words here are tend to and generally. The research doesn't suggest that all men are agentic, nor that all women are communal.

A meta-analysis of 162 separate leadership studies found that men tend to be more autocratic and directive, whereas women tend to be more democratic and participative[12]. Out of a choice of Transformational, Transactional and Laissez-faire leadership styles, women will tend to be much more Transformational in their style[13]. Interestingly, where women do use a more Transactional and assertive style, even within it they tend to use more positive and rewarding language and strategies compared to men, who tend to use more negative and threatening strategies and language[14]. Recent research suggests that the most effective leadership style sits in the middle ground between being participative and directive[15]. Consistent with my proposition in Chapter 1, could this be an argument for leadership balance, where the best leaders sit comfortably in the middle of the People/Task, Empathising/Systemising continuums, but with the flexibility to move up and down the scales, as the situation and circumstances require it?

Unfortunately, as is so often the case with research where the answer isn't clear, other studies show contradictory rather than confirmatory evidence. In contrast to the previous research finding that there is a difference in the way that men and women lead, a 2010 study found no significant gender differences between male and female German managers where culturally, a Transformational leadership style was preferred[16]. A subsequent 2011 research study also found no significant gender differences either between the management and leadership styles of public sector managers in Sweden[17]. These findings do rather beg the questions though as to whether it was gendered leadership which was being explored by these studies, or rather cultural differences in leadership style between the UK and Europe, and whether the level which was investigated is also significant. Might there be a difference between middle management and senior leadership in terms of style?

But this isn't the whole picture. There are other, invisible factors implicitly present in the gendered leadership domain that are also relevant to the debate. Have you heard of 'the glass cliff' or 'the glass escalator'? Analysis of UK companies confirms that a senior woman executive tends to be appointed in situations where, historically, performance has been poor, or where the leadership position itself is precarious[18], leading to the term 'glass cliff'. In comparison, a man is more likely to experience an almost invisible pressure to be promoted upwards in traditionally female roles such as nursing and teaching, even if they do not actively pursue advancement. There seems to be an imperceptible underlying assumption that higher status roles, with greater responsibility and of course, a higher salary, should be theirs[19], as if they are standing on an invisible glass escalator and being propelled upwards.

Where a woman displays more agentic and masculine traits, she is less likely to be appointed. She is even less likely to be appointed if she is perceived as being aggressive or status enhancing, i.e. less communal and classically feminine[20]. The same behaviours that are accepted in a man and will enhance his status will be penalised in a woman[21]. This situation of hostile stereotyping, is also true when, for example, a women tries to negotiate greater compensation. Unlike a man, she will generally be disliked for it[22]. Is it any wonder then that a recognisable gender pay-gap exists within the UK so that women, on average, receive less remuneration than a man does, for fulfilling the same role[23]?

Hostile sexism is the explanation given to the blatant bullying of women in traditionally male environments such as construction and engineering. For some reason it appears to be acceptable to some men to subject female colleagues to aggressive verbal, physical and sexual behaviours they would not find tolerable if those same behaviours were directed at their own wives, sisters or mothers. No Authentic Leader would ever behave in such a way, or would even entertain such thoughts, attitudes or behaviours as being in any way appropriate. I can only think that these men are particularly susceptible to feelings of status threat and to the effects of testosterone and power. What happens to culture within these organisations when such men are promoted?

As promised earlier, let's think about social and cultural influence. Prior to seeing a particular media advert, both male and female students expressed equal interest in taking on a leadership role once they had finished their studies. After viewing an advert in which the leadership role was portrayed by a man, the female students expressed less interest in choosing to have a leadership role. The same effect was found after the advert portrayed the woman as ditsy or in a traditional domestic, housewife role[24]. How can a simple advert affect the career aspirations of an intelligent woman? The answer is stereotype threat. Where our natural inclination is to think or behave in ways which do not match the social and culturally accepted stereotypes, our very psyche is threatened, unconsciously leading us to try to fit in with the stereotypes, even if we consciously reject them.

In an emerging leaders' study, some interesting findings were uncovered. In both laboratory and real leadership situations, in initially leaderless groups where the groups and team working was going to be short-term, in situations which didn't require complex social interactions, and in predominantly task-oriented situations, male leadership emerged as the most likely outcome. In contrast however, where the objectives were slightly longer-term, more complex and where social relationships were likely to affect the outcomes, women tended to emerge as leaders to a greater extent than men[25].

Remember, this research isn't suggesting that in 100% of cases, complex and social group requirements mean that female leadership will emerge, or that short-term and task-focused objectives means the emergence of male leadership; however, it is a thought-provoking study.

Maybe we can make more sense of it if we turn it on its head. Perhaps it is the more relational, people-focused leadership style that is more effective in longer-term, complex, non-urgent, socially rich environments, whereas in shorter-term and more urgent situations and more task-focused environments, it is the more directive, task-oriented approach that is the most effective, *regardless of the gender of the leader*. This would certainly be true of Coastguard rescues, where the most effective leadership style in the Coastguard Station is a relational one, and where the leadership style switches immediately to a hierarchical approach as the most effective style literally the second the alarm is raised. The major concern for leadership development in the Coastguard, as it is in the military, then becomes one of the situational and environmental flexibility of its leaders to be able to adapt their leadership style between the two scenarios. Issues emerge when a predominantly directive leader cannot become relational and vice-versa: both are problematic and ultimately destructive.

Why don't women-only shortlists work?

Apart from the fact that in 1996 they were ruled to be illegal under the Sex Discrimination Act of 1975, one of the most important elements in the women's equality debate is: what kind of gender equality are we talking about? Do we want equality of opportunity, i.e. where anyone can apply if they think they are good enough; or do we want equality of outcome? i.e. where there is an equal gender split of men and women on Boards and in Parliament. By using women-preferred shortlists, we cannot, by definition, have equality of opportunity, if male candidates are discriminated against.

Equality of opportunity isn't the only issue here. Did you notice that I deliberately wrote, 'anyone can apply if they think they are good enough'. We now know that men and women generally rate themselves differently regarding their competence. In another meta-analysis of more than 95 studies, researchers found that there was no difference in the way that followers rated their male and female bosses: both were thought to perform equally as well. However, the male leaders themselves generally thought that they were better than their peers and over-rated themselves, whereas the women were more modest and generally under-rated themselves[26]. In a culture that values confidence, is it any wonder that a woman is less likely than a man to put herself forward for promotion or to demand equal pay for doing the same job?

Here, once again, women are at a disadvantage. Men are more confident applying for roles that they are qualified for than women are. In fact, men are much more confident in applying for roles that they are not quite qualified for! Women are much less likely to apply for a role that they are qualified for, until they are 100% qualified, or even over-qualified for it; only then will they apply[27].

Female quotas, currently popular in the UK, have been instrumental in getting more women appointed to Board positions. However, all of the Senior Executive women I have met, and over the years I have met a great many of them, want to be appointed to a Board position because of the quality of their thinking and because of what they can offer, not because of tokenism or because they possess breasts and a vagina. From this perspective, female quotas and women-preferred shortlists are, at their worst, insulting to women and they offend both genders.

So over the past 20 years, there has been an increasing focus on trying to identify how women lead comparative to men. Perhaps because research both supports gendered leadership stereotypes and refutes them, there haven't really been any meaningful conclusions. We could say that this is surprising considering how much time, effort and resources have been invested to date. Yet from another perspective, the confusion of these findings isn't really a surprise at all. As I said earlier, the whole gendered leadership debate as it is currently conceived is an enormous red herring and it's no wonder that, for a variety of reasons, female quotas and women-preferred shortlists don't necessarily work in terms of diversity and balancing the approach and outcomes of Boards.

> *We don't need diversity of gender in the Boardroom,*
> *we need diversity of thinking[28].*

What's the solution?

We are already slowly beginning to experience a culture shift towards a more balanced leadership style as seen in Europe[29]. We need to become more consciously aware of such things as unconscious bias, stereotypes and stereotype threats, so that we see the person and not their gender. The more openness and transparency there is regarding equal payment for a role regarding salary, terms and conditions and bonuses, the less hostile reactions there will be by those who are particularly affected by power and concerns of status. We also need to stop seeing people like Jack Welch and Steve Jobs as acceptable, or worse, aspirational, leadership role models. They aren't. Both had deeply flawed leadership styles which damaged the well-being of many people, as we will go on to explore in Chapter 7 when we consider leadership derailers and the dark side of leadership.

If we know that some men 'think like women', and some women 'think like men', then judging people by their gender becomes as ridiculous as the Victorians measuring head size. Therefore, and rather obviously, we also need to understand the thinking style profiles of the people we appoint to senior positions in a more effective way than we currently do.

Whilst it may have a part to play, we cannot continue to use gender as the major factor that drives leadership style or leadership selection. By promulgating gendered leadership we have been viewing leadership through the wrong lens. Not only don't gender stereotypes work anymore, (if they ever did), gendered leadership stereotypes don't work either. We have to find another way, and I have come to the belief that I have found one.

I'm proposing that we take a biological look at personality and leadership[30]. Considering the influence that dopamine, oestrogen, testosterone and serotonin have on our thinking, personality, behaviours and our leadership styles provides us with a much more meaningful and useful perspective on leadership and management. A more balanced perspective, which is beneficial for us as leaders and for those who are led and managed by us, is the result.

The next chapter introduces the four Leadership Temperament Types to you. We will learn about the dopamine-driven Charismatic Explorer; the oestrogen-driven Relational Negotiator; the testosterone-driven Transactional Director and the serotonin-driven Transformational Builder.

Chapter 3: Leadership Temperament Types

As I mentioned earlier, the American anthropologist Dr Helen Fisher was the first person I encountered who theorised the possibility that biological drivers might influence our personality and behaviours. As a biological anthropologist, she was interested in human relationships, specifically romantic mate selection preferences, and her work on Temperament Types was used by both Chemistry.com and Match.com to help them develop their formulas for pairing up potential romantic partners[1].

I found her theory fascinating and I wondered whether there was a way of relating her ideas to what we know, and, of course, what we don't know, about leadership. It's a subject which continues to fascinate us now as much as it interested the Greeks and Romans centuries ago. I was doing my doctoral research into Authentic Leadership at the time I came across Dr Fisher's work and the more I thought about it, the more my own theories and ideas about the possibility of Leadership Temperament Types began to take shape. After an exchange of emails between us, I called Dr Fisher in the States and she agreed that she thought I was definitely on to something.

First, I'm going to describe the two Leadership Temperament Types which you are most likely to recognise as the classically male and female stereotypes, which of course we now know from Chapters 1 and 2 are not really determined by gender at all. However, as heuristics, and because they will already be familiar to you, we are going to utilise them. These are the testosterone-driven Director and the oestrogen-driven Negotiator. I will then go on to explain the two lesser well known and understood Leadership Temperament Types of the Explorer and the Builder. You will probably recognise all of them in the people that you know or have worked with.

The percentage figures that I'm going to share with you regarding the numbers of people who have self-reported a primary preference for each temperament type have been taken from Fisher's work, published in her book on relationships: *Why Him, Why Her?*[1]. However, it's important to remember a couple of things about these figures: firstly, these % statistics are North American figures rather than UK ones, although at more than 40,000 people, the population sample is so big that we can reasonably assume that UK figures would be similar; and secondly, the population sample Fisher used was a general population sample rather than a managerial or leadership one. This means that if we were only to use leaders within the sample population, the percentage figures that would emerge for each Leadership Temperament Type would probably be different. You will understand why I say this when you understand more about the Leadership Temperament Types and the effect of testosterone in particular on leadership style.

Before we begin exploring the four Leadership Temperament Types in more depth there are some things that it's important to understand about the theory. Remember that, despite the existence of some supporting evidence, and despite Fisher putting it forward as a new way of conceptualising personality[2], at the moment it's just a working model that seems to make intuitive and practical sense. It makes sense in both the areas of romantic relationships, (Fisher's area of expertise), and leadership, (my area of expertise). It's not proven like gravity, it's simply a new model of behaviours, thinking and motivational drivers which I'm sharing with you because it seems to explain why some people rise to the top of organisations where the power is, and others don't. It helps us to understand why we have some of the gender stereotypes that we do around male and female thinking and behaviours, and it will help you to understand your place in the world and possibly your role within it. It's not a panacea, it's just something useful and interesting to know that will help you to understand yourself and other people better. In this complicated and sometimes difficult world that we live in, that surely has to be a good thing.

Fisher suggests that we have a primary and secondary preference regarding the temperament types and that this is the most important thing to pay attention to. That may or may not be true for romantic relationships, I don't know. My thinking, as a psychologist rather than as an anthropologist, is slightly different, which is why, in Chapter 5, and on the book's website, *www.unitedbychocolate.com*, I've designed the diagnostic questionnaires and reports in the way that I have. I have come to believe that all of the Leadership Temperament Types are important; both in the order of preference that we experience them, and also in the percentage level that we have for each of them.

I find the theory of Leadership Temperament Types really exciting for two reasons: firstly, it makes intuitive sense and it provides a useful working model of what appears to be going on in Boardrooms around the world; and, secondly, it's brand new! Whilst Fisher's theory of Temperament Types has been around for a few years, when I spoke with her she confirmed that no one has linked it to leadership styles before, nor to Authentic Leadership, so you really are reading all about it here first! Many years ago, in the early 1970s, when I was about seven years old and in primary school, we were taught about the theory of plate tectonics, which, at the time, was also a relatively new theory, as it was dismissed in the 1920s and then re-visited in the 1960s. I remember specifically that our class teacher was very excited about it. That's how I feel about the theory of Leadership Temperament Types. Maybe one day, and sooner rather than later, Leadership Temperament Types will become mainstream thinking and simply accepted as common sense and obvious once people understand how the pieces of the jigsaw puzzle fit together, in the same way that tectonic plates fit together.

So let's begin to explore the four Leadership Temperament Types, using the labels which Fisher uses. They are: Directors, Negotiators, Explorers, and Builders.

Directors

As the name suggests, Directors like to be directive! However, it's not as simple as that; we need to consider the underlying reasons which give rise to that particular behaviour. Biologically, the chemical which drives Directors is the hormone testosterone, and while Chapter 4 goes into more depth regarding the effects of testosterone on mood and behaviour, it is worth exploring it briefly here too, especially as you will undoubtedly recognise some of the things associated with it.

Testosterone makes people more focused; it enables concentrated attention for a sustained period of time. In order to be able to do this, a Director will filter out what they perceive to be unnecessary or unimportant information and details. Sometimes they won't hear you, or will seem to ignore you; sometimes they may forget to eat, so engrossed are they on the task at hand. I use the word 'task' deliberately, as one of the most striking characteristics of the Director is just how task-focused they can be when something engages their attention. When it does, they will pursue it with an unswerving focus, often ignoring anything that doesn't assist them in achieving their goals.

This task focus of the Director not only makes them appear driven; testosterone has a few other behavioural effects. One of the other things it does, which you will no doubt be familiar with, is make people competitive. There is an enormous drive to win, to beat the competition, sometimes it seems, at any cost[3]. Are you beginning to recognise anyone you know? Possibly even yourself?

Being goal-oriented, competitive, focused and driven to win goes hand-in-hand with a number of other Director behaviours and traits. Having testosterone as an underlying hormonal driver also changes people's use of language; it makes them use words and phrases which are much more "I", "me" oriented. High testosterone levels are correlated with a reduced use of words related to social connections, other people, and importantly, a concern for others. In other words, higher levels of testosterone seem to make people much more self-focused, often to the point where they can appear cold, disinterested in other people and selfish[4]. This would fit well with the People/Task Continuum we explored in Chapter 1.

To summarise so far, we are beginning to meet in the Director someone who is focused, driven, directive, competitive, self-focused and very likely to succeed. Does this in any way remind you of the stereotypical, agentic, masculine leader we met in Chapter 2?

Let's continue to explore some more likely Director traits and behaviours because there is a depth to this kind of person that can sometimes be missed if we only look at the surface. I find some of the research around testosterone fascinating. Having spoken to many people I would classify as predominantly Directors, both male and female, one of the things which strikes me about them isn't how much they are driven to win, but how much they hate to lose. We will explore more about this in Chapter 4, but there is research to suggest that the testosterone spike when someone wins is much less than the corresponding testosterone dip when they lose. So powerful is this effect, it can be seen and measured in the testosterone levels of the fans in the winning and losing teams of the football FA Cup Final[5]. Losing will make the Director much more focused and they will regroup and redouble their efforts in the future to ensure success and avoid losing again. They will be ruthless in this, and if you cannot help them to succeed, you will be dropped from their team. It isn't personal, but if you can't help them to win, they simply won't want you around.

One of the things that can make Directors easy to work with is that they are so straight-forward and forthright. They will say what they mean and mean what they say. They will want you to get straight to the point and to focus on the facts rather than how you may feel about something. They will often describe themselves as being realistic and pragmatic. They are outwardly objective, confident, emotionally contained to the point of being detached, tough-minded, resilient and logical.

Logic and rationality are two things that the Director values very highly. They are often intellectually rigorous and there's nothing they like better than stimulating debate. Dr Helen Fisher describes them as wanting to find a 'mind mate' in their most significant personal relationship, and in the world of work this will often translate into their seeking out colleagues they can bounce intellectual ideas around with, or even a sparring partner. Sometimes the downside to this, combined with their recognised drive, competitiveness and lack of sensitivity, is that they can come across as intellectual bullies, who throw their intellectual weight around in order to achieve their own aims, regardless of who they hurt in the process and the trail of hurt they may leave in their wake. I have met many of them, both men and women, in the world of business and commerce and also in academia, all domains where they thrive and will build empires if they can.

Fiercely ambitious, driven by power and a need to be in control, focused and competent, it's no wonder then that Directors often rise to the top of departments and organisations. According to Fisher, 24.8% of men have Director as their first temperament type preference, although only 9.7% of women do. So that's one in four men and one in ten women within the general population who are likely to be fairly easily identifiable as Directors because of their first temperament type preference. You will undoubtedly have met some of them. You may even be one yourself.

From the perspective of gender stereotypes, these percentage figures make perfect sense, don't they? Remember though that they are taken from a general population sample of ordinary working age people and were not taken from a specific leadership group sample.   As I mentioned earlier, I strongly suspect, when the research is eventually done, that because Directors actively seek, and so often have, a leadership role, if we were only to profile leaders, we would find that the percentage of senior leaders who have a Director profile as their first and predominant preference would be significantly higher, for both men and women.

Negotiators

In many ways, the 'opposite' of the Director is the Negotiator. I use the word opposite carefully though, because of course Negotiators are not really the opposite of Directors. However, as a mental framework, it can be useful to think of them in this way as it simplifies the Leadership Temperament Types model. You will be able to see this quite easily if you look on the grid diagram later on in this chapter.

Just as Directors are driven by testosterone, in comparison, the underlying biological hormonal driver for a Negotiator is oestrogen.

Oestrogen is the nurturing hormone and Negotiators are powerfully driven by the quality of their relationships with others. Negotiators are compassionate and warm, caring and interested in other people, and they will always try to find a workable solution which everyone is happy with. Unlike Directors, they do not weigh things up objectively and logically, but rather, they will always take a people-focused approach and will want to consider things from all angles, taking a multi-perspective approach to problem solving which involves the thoughts and feelings of everybody involved. This can make them appear less focused than the Director and obviously their multiple perspective strategy takes more time, so they may appear less decisive and results oriented by comparison. Don't be fooled by their warmth though, they can be just as brave and passionate in their decision making as the Director is, and just as committed to the outcomes and results, just so long as no-one is harmed on the way to achieving them.

Hormonally speaking, oestrogen makes people trusting, kind, empathetic and interested in the well-being of others. Genuine, open and honest, Negotiators will prefer to avoid confrontation and difficult situations if possible. Challenging others or being challenged by them can make the Negotiator feel very uncomfortable. They are much more likely to take a facilitative role at work rather than one which requires definitive action and driving things through. Because of this, a Negotiator will prefer a more gentle and collaborative approach to the full-on frontal attack often favoured by the Director.

Oestrogen enables the Negotiator to tolerate ambiguity relatively easily. It also facilitates high levels of trust in them regarding the people they work with, especially as they like to think the best of everyone. This does mean of course that they can sometimes have their good nature abused by people who are not like them; that is, other people who are not Negotiators! This is usually something they recognise and you may find that at work, they may hide or disguise their true natures to avoid being taken advantage of.

While the Director really hates losing, the Negotiator has an aversion to superficiality; they like nothing better than deep and meaningful conversations, especially if they are able to make a positive difference to someone's life through their words, their actions or their emotional support. Oestrogen also facilitates the ability to be charitable and forgiving, generally agreeable, flexible and open. They respond to genuine and heartfelt dialogue and seek authenticity from their friends. Fisher suggests that in their primary romantic partnerships, more than anything else, they really desire a 'soul mate'.

Fisher suggests that 20.4% of men in the general population have Negotiator as their first Temperament Type preference, which is one in five men, compared to 35.8% of women. This means that, broadly speaking, approximately almost double the number of women have Negotiator as their predominant preference type compared to men. This would fit well with the female stereotypes we explored in Chapters 1 and 2. No wonder then that we expect women, and female managers and leaders, to be kind and considerate, nurturing and caring, and we notice when they aren't.

Explorers

As their name suggests, Explorers like to explore the world and everything in it! They are spontaneous, energetic, optimistic and playful. They are very exciting to be around and they will infuse you with their enthusiasm and their ideas. Sometimes these ideas can appear rather 'out there' and 'off-the-wall', as Explorers can be amazingly creative; but once again, don't be fooled, there will be a nugget in their idea, a kernel of something that most other people haven't seen. Sometimes, with a bit of luck and a fair wind behind them, their ideas can completely change the way that we think about things.

Fisher suggests that within the general population one in four people will be an Explorer; the figures are very balanced across the sexes, with 27.1% of men and 25.1% of women self-reporting that they have Explorer as their first Temperament Type preference. The underlying biology for the Explorer is the neurotransmitter dopamine, which is associated with restlessness and sensation seeking as well as a desire for novelty. I suspect, although I only have anecdotal evidence for it so far, that men and women may express their Explorer preferences slightly differently. Whilst all of them may be spontaneous, energetic, creative and playful, it seems that men, more than women, use sport and outdoor adventure to fulfil their Explorer natures, whether that's overland adventuring in a Land Rover which keeps breaking down, or fell running and taking part in the Spine Race, an expedition race in the UK where you have to run an ultra-marathon every day for a week. Explorers are quite easy to spot when you know what you are looking for! I can hear you asking what women Explorers do; it seems that they get creative, take manageable, rather than major, risks, and often set up small businesses. They seem to integrate their adventures into their daily lives rather than keeping them separate and having one big hobby which they do with a group of friends. This may have something to do with women being the predominant childcare and elder-care providers in society. Perhaps if you are an Explorer you will go onto the book's website at *www.unitedbychocolate.com* and share with other readers what you do and how you fulfil your Explorer tendencies!

Dopamine activation is linked to playing down danger and therefore involvement in risky or even high-risk activities. When we consider that dopamine activates testosterone, it's easy to make the connection to all kinds of risky activities, both competitive and non-competitive, that the Explorer might engage in, either personally or professionally. I'm thinking here about sports such as bungee and base jumping, parachuting, white water rafting, risky or exciting dating, driving too fast, drinking too much or betting and gaming. At work, having dopamine as a driver could translate into a preference for risky or personally exciting projects, sales, deals of some kind or out-of-the-box proposals which haven't been tried before and scientific research. I've chosen my words very carefully here because one person's exciting could be another person's risky, and it's important not to assume that any one temperament type is somehow 'better' than any other.

Within their most significant personal relationship, Fisher suggests that what Explorers most desire is a 'play mate'. In terms of a working role, it's easy to understand how jobs such as being in the fire service, the police or being a paramedic where every day is different and the unknown is around every corner, possibly involving danger, could appeal to the Explorer.

Builders

As I'm writing this for you, at home in the July of 2015, with a surprise summer shower raining down outside and our family corgi dog by my feet, twitching in her dreams as she chases rabbits through the fields outside, I've just had a phone call from the architect who's building the new garage and office for me in the garden. We had a conversation about building safe and stable futures for our respective children, and about loyalty and the duty he feels to his family and also to his clients. These are exactly the kinds of things that make life meaningful to Builders. They value stability, safety and sustainability very highly, as they do family and traditions.

Builders make lifelong friends and often see themselves as the guardians of their communities. They are completely reliable and you will frequently find them volunteering in support of local projects. They are honourable, prudent, dutiful, compliant and patient. Of all of the four temperament types, Builders are probably the most ethically oriented, as they think deeply about the consequences and implications which decisions and actions taken now will have on the future. They can sometimes come across as being risk-averse, overly cautious or resisting change, but in reality perhaps they are none of those things; they may just appear that way in comparison to Explorers or Directors. A Builder will be concerned that sometimes, in their haste to get things done and succeed, and in their desire for management and control, the Director can overlook important information and the similarly, the Explorer can under-estimate risks which the Builder sees as relevant and important to the issues at hand.

The Builder can therefore sometimes be thought of as the brakes of a proposal or plan; there to ensure health and safety and the ongoing success and sustainability of the project in the longer term. They like to build things that last. Solid foundations – that's the Builder. The underlying biology which drives the Builder is the neurotransmitter serotonin. This is interesting, because within the body's endocrinology, serotonin is a moderator, which enables many of the other hormones and chemicals in the body to function more effectively. Moderation is something which the Builder finds very attractive, in all areas of their lives. Fisher suggests that in their most significant romantic relationship, Builders want to find a 'help mate', a special person who can assist them in building something worthwhile and lasting for the future, probably with a long-term responsibility for others built into it. Fisher suggests that people with a Builder profile as their primary temperament type are most likely to marry young and are least likely to divorce.

The Link to Chocolate

Serotonin is released into the bloodstream when we eat carbohydrates like bread and potatoes. It is also produced and released when we consume that most delicious of sweet treats: chocolate. So if you know someone who is particularly fond of any or all of these serotonin-releasing foods, just consider for a moment that they may be a serotonin-driven Builder! This is where the title of the book comes from; as human beings we are undoubtedly biologically divided by gender. However, if you look at the figures, you will realise that we are most definitely united by chocolate.

According to Fisher's data, the gender split for men and women whose first temperament type preference is the Builder is 27.6% for men, and 29.4% for women in a general population sample. This means that, broadly speaking, on average, every one in three people you meet at work is likely to be the patient, reliable, trustworthy and pro-social Builder; although, of course, that may depend slightly on the industry and environment that you work in. High tech start-ups, for example, may have a higher proportion of Explorers in them!

Diagram 3 presents a summary overview of each of the four Leadership Temperament Types. You will notice that in the bullet point summaries, it appears that Director behaviours tend to be the opposite of the Negotiator ones, just as Builder preferences seem to be the opposite of the Explorer ones. This is partly because I wanted to simplify things for you so it will be easier for you to remember the theory and partly because I really enjoy the symmetry and clarity of the model. For me, it has a beauty and elegance to it. I hope that at least some of you will feel the same way about it, although, of course, the Directors amongst you will be more sceptical!

I expect that as you read Diagram 3 you will either, mentally in your head, or physically with a pen, make a note of which bullet points are true for you. There are a couple of interesting things to highlight for you while you are doing that. Some of you will find that you have a very clear overall preference for one kind of behaviour or set of behaviours compared to its opposite in the grid. This makes diagnosis and understanding very clear and straight forward. However, some of you may find that both of the statements on each side of the page are true of you, to some degree. This is because none of the temperament types are mutually exclusive; if you are particularly flexible, it will depend on your situation and circumstances as well as your motivation and desired outcomes as to which strategies you will apply.

There are a couple of other things that I need to mention about Diagram 3. Some of the characteristics I've described have been deliberately put in inverted commas. This is because they are not really true! However, they may appear to be true to someone who doesn't share that preference. So, for example, Builders are not really 'dull' and 'boring'; however, they may appear so to an Explorer. By the same token, Explorers are not really 'reckless'. However, a Builder might see their risky activities and describe them as such! My intention, in this book, is to describe the thinking and behaviours of each temperament type not ascribe a value judgement to them!

You will also notice that in Diagram 3 I have associated each temperament type with a recognised leadership style. All of these four leadership styles: Charismatic, Relational, Transactional and Transformational, already exist within the literature, and while they may not be an exact match to the theory of Leadership Temperament Types, at least in so far as the academic research to date, there are enough similarities between them for us to be able to use them as an appropriate fit.

Chapter 5 invites you to answer some diagnostic questionnaires that include more details so that you can calculate your personal preferences for each temperament type. However, you can use the bullet-point summaries in Diagram 3 here in this chapter to begin to work out your likely predominant Leadership Temperament Type preference as well as how much of each of the Types you might be.

Relational Negotiators	**Transactional Directors**
• People focused	• Task focused
• Warm and caring	• Cold and dispassionate
• Collaborative	• Competitive
• Value relationships	• Value success
• Comfortable with ambiguity	• Need things clearly defined
• An extreme 'female' brain?	• An extreme 'male' brain?
• Need intimacy and connectedness	• Need intellectual stimulation
• Hate superficiality	• Hate losing
29.1% of the general population of which 20.4% are men, and 35.8% are women [1]	*16.3% of the general population of which 24.8% are men, and 9.7% are women* [1]

Charismatic Explorers	**Transformational Builders**
• Risk and thrill seeking	• Risk averse and cautious
• Innovative and unconventional	• Traditional and conventional
• Likely to change their minds	• Consistent and reliable
• Charismatic and exciting	• 'Dull' and 'boring'
• 'Reckless'	• Cautious
• May have flexible ethics	• Staunchly ethical and moral
• Need adrenalin and excitement	• Need stability and familiarity
• Hate being bored	• Hate dishonesty
26% of general population of which 27.1% are men, and 25.1% are women [1]	*28.6% of general population of which 27.6% are men, and 29.4% are women* [1]

[1] Data taken from Dr Helen Fisher's book, *Why Him, Why Her?* Note that these figures are taken from a general population sample of 40,000 North Americans who were using the *Chemistry.com* dating website.

Chapter 4: Biology and the Link to Values

This chapter needs to begin with a number of caveats. Firstly, I am a social scientist, not a medical one so I'm not an endocrinologist. However, Dr Helen Fisher is a biological anthropologist, and she has used both psychometric questionnaires and also MRI neuroimaging of the brain to identify supporting evidence for the existence of the four Temperament Types and the thinking and behaviours associated with them[1]. In the explanations given here I have necessarily simplified things so that the findings and the research are related to leadership behaviours and are readable at the same time, so if you are a medical practitioner I apologise in advance for any over-simplification.

Secondly, our endocrinology is a very complex chemical soup. Just as our biological hormones can influence our thoughts and feelings, our language and behaviours, (ask any woman who has ever menstruated), so too can our thoughts, feelings and experience influence our hormone and neurotransmitter levels. This will become even more apparent when we go on to explore testosterone, cortisol and the winner effect later on in the chapter.

Thirdly, the truth is that our endocrine system is so complex in the way that the hormones are secreted, regulated and combined in the body with other chemicals, that no one really knows all that much about why they affect us in the ways that they do. There are a number of reasons for this: experimental studies are done on rodents, birds and monkeys rather than humans; there are different kinds of serotonin, for example, which appear to act differently even though they are all serotonin; and the same hormone at the same dosage will affect individuals differently for some reason, with some people being more susceptible to certain hormonal influences than others[2].

Foetal testosterone is being promulgated by a few researchers, such as Baron-Cohen to support his theories regarding the gendered male/female brain, but as we've already discussed in Chapter 2, and as the case studies in Chapter 9 clearly show, the male/female brain theory linked as an absolute to gender is fundamentally flawed, with foetal and child/adult development being much more complex than Baron-Cohen's simple continuum allows for. For this reason, while I support the gendered brain as a useful model and respect the brilliant work which Baron-Cohen and his colleagues have done regarding their observations and research on the autistic spectrum, I am yet to be convinced regarding the arguments for foetal testosterone being the determining factor in an individual's Systemising/Empathising and People/Task preferences. This is not least because the foetal testosterone theory seems to completely ignore subsequent environmental factors and also the fundamental principles of brain plasticity, cognitive flexibility and individual agency in choosing how to think and behave. This is one of the nature/nurture debates which will undoubtedly continue until we understand much more than we currently do about the human body and its endocrinology in particular.

Finally, it is worth remembering that we have a myriad of chemicals circulating around our bodies all of the time at different levels and it would be a nonsense to suggest that we are only influenced by four of them. While there is supporting evidence from Fisher and other researchers linking our biology and our Temperament Types together as primary underpinning motivational drivers[3], I would suggest that the most useful approach is to view the theory of Leadership Temperament Types as a mental framework around which to pin our thoughts and ideas.

Dopamine

Dopamine is synthesised both in the body and in the brain. In the brain it's a neurotransmitter and there are recognised dopamine pathways associated with reward-motivated behaviours. Many addictive drugs are implicated in the increase of neurological dopamine activity in the brain. Dopamine has been correlated with sensation seeking, excitement, novelty and new experience, having a low boredom threshold and lack of restraint[4]. It's also implicated in addictive behaviours such as gambling[5]. Dopamine is synthesised in the body by the adrenal glands, and is closely associated with noradrenaline. Adrenaline increases alertness and focused attention in times of heightened arousal and can lead to impulsive behaviour as it reduces the perception of risk, thereby increasing risk-taking and involvement in potentially dangerous activities. Dopamine activation stimulates the neural reward pathways when both risky activities and pleasurable events are experienced.

The adrenal glands, situated just above the kidneys, also synthesise the stress hormone cortisol, stimulated by the anterior lobe of the pituitary gland. Cortisol interferes with the production of serotonin and dopamine, both of which, as neurotransmitters, are involved in the stability of mood and feelings of wellness. This suggests that like the Builder and the testosterone-driven Director, potentially, the Explorer may also find stressful events more difficult to cope with than the Negotiator, who appears to be protected from the effects of stress by oestrogen[6].

Researchers have associated dopamine with novelty-seeking, impulsiveness and extravagance[7]. By using modern technologies such as magnetic resonance imaging (MRI) scans, dopamine and its neural reward pathways have been linked to curiosity and a desire to explore, both physically, and intellectually[8]. Originality, the generation of abstract or concrete ideas, and both physical and linguistic creativity, are also associated with dopamine activity[9]. Perhaps that's one of the reasons why many of us find creative activities so pleasurable and rewarding, and why it's so important that for adults, as well as for children, to allow ourselves time to play, whatever that may mean for us.

Oestrogen

Whilst oestrogen is recognised as the primary sex hormone that's responsible for the 'femaleness' and 'femininity' of someone, oestrogen is actually synthethised from androgens, specifically testosterone and androstenedione. Both sexes produce oestrogen, and both men and women require it as it's associated with, amongst other things, bone formation, protein synthesis, coagulation, melanin, lung function, sexual desire and libido.

Baron-Cohen has linked verbal fluency and other language skills with oestrogen priming in the womb. This contrasts with higher levels of testosterone, which has been shown to correlate with reduced language skills in pre-school children, particularly boys[10]. Oestrogen is associated with being empathetic, sympathetic, with acts of kindness, nurturing others and pro-social relationship skills at an individual level[11]. The ability to manage ambiguity and mental flexibility are also associated with oestrogen activity[12].

Interestingly, it seems that oestrogen may have a protective function against the effects of stress[13]. Researchers, admittedly working with male and female rats rather than people, put the rodents through a series of tasks designed to mimic human stressors such as being cognitively challenged by complexity, being under time pressure, having to multi-task, short-term memory experiments and tasks specifically designed to frustrate. They discovered a number of things that surprised them. First, they found that the females were more resilient to chronic stress, that is, stress over the longer term. The male rats suffered much more from stress and this led to problems for them with their short-term memory and with multi-tasking. They also became more frustrated than the female rats, more short-tempered and were more likely to suffer from angry or aggressive outbursts.

An inability to remember a familiar object when stressed, such as experienced by the male rats, indicates a disturbance in the parts of the brain which are responsible for higher-level, 'executive' processes such as decision-making and managing multiple tasks and projects. Repeated, ongoing stress in the male rats resulted in permanent damage to their brains in the areas associated with this higher cognitive functioning. When non-brain-damaged male rats were exposed to higher levels of oestrogen, their ability to cope with stress improved to the same levels as the female rats. Conversely, when the female rats had the oestrogen signalling in their brains blocked, they became just as susceptible to the stressful effects and angry outbursts as the males. One of the really interesting findings of the study was that even the female rats that had had their ovaries removed were still protected from stress. This suggests that it is the oestrogen that is produced by the brain which is the protective oestrogen element. Both male and female rodents produce oestrogen, just as male and female humans do, and this finding is significant in suggesting that oestrogen protection generated from within the brain is not gender specific. After all, a female rat with no ovaries is the hormonal equivalent of a male from an oestrogen perspective.

The implications of this research from the perspective of Leadership Temperament Types are significant, especially if we link it to Baron-Cohen's extreme male brain theory in Chapter 1. It suggests that as oestrogen is also produced in the brain, it is not gender specific; i.e., an oestrogen brain dominance that subsequently drives behaviour may not be exclusively female. Critically, it also means that the Negotiators, with their more Relational leadership style may be much better at multi-tasking and dealing with the kind of workplace stressors which I've described. Conversely, it also means that potentially, the testosterone-driven Directors, with their Transactional, task focused leadership style, may be less able to cope with these stressors. Certainly this might go some way towards explaining the angry and sometimes even violent outbursts which the testosterone-driven Director can sometimes have, and why, when they become stressed, they have a tendency towards heightened focus and it seems as if they cannot cope with more than one thing at a time.

Testosterone

The hormone testosterone is responsible for the 'maleness' of someone. Physically it's associated with muscle and bone mass, body hair, strength, energy, sexual drive, voice tone, sustained cognitive focus and physical and mental endurance. It's predominantly secreted by the testes in men and the ovaries in women, and to a lesser extent in small amounts by the adrenal glands. It's one of the hormones which we are most familiar with, possibly because it's readily measureable in saliva, meaning that research around baseline levels and fluctuations can be easily done. It's commonly associated with socially dominant, even aggressive, male behaviour[14]. Researchers investigating levels of testosterone and aggression in prison inmates found that the men who committed sex crimes had significantly higher baseline levels of testosterone than those who committed property crime[15].

Testosterone is linked to independence and emotional containment[16]. It's also implicated in having less social sensitivity towards others and to emotional flooding, particularly anger and rage[17]. It seems to be the hormone responsible for being able to sustain mental and physical energy over long periods of time and for decreased levels of exhaustion. It also has an association with power. Researchers have shown that not only does having power and feeling in control allow us to focus our attention, it also means that we are less likely to be put off by distractions. This is useful in terms of being able to be productive. However, the downside of attentional focus is attentional deficit: Directors literally do not see or hear the linguistic, behavioural or situational clues which, in a Negotiator and Builder, would be the early warning signs that something was going awry and needed attention[18].

Not only do hormones shape and change our behaviour, our behaviour changes our hormones. Winning causes surges in testosterone. It makes animals more aggressive, less anxious and more confident. It increases their pain threshold and makes them more likely to win again in the future[19]. In a famous 1994 football study when Italy played Brazil in the FIFA World Cup Final, researchers took saliva samples to measure the testosterone levels in the fans when their team won or lost. There was an average rise in testosterone of 28% in the winning team supporters and a decrease of 27% in the fans of the losing team. Researchers had difficulty tracking down the losing Italian fans; they had effectively gone into hiding to lick their wounds, so badly did they feel about losing[20].

Having higher basal levels of testosterone may well account for what is probably one of the most interesting things regarding Transactional Director's Leadership behaviours. It seems that there are two kinds of testosterone-driven Directors. The first kind, a leader like Jack Welch, is highly competitive, socially dominant, aggressive, hates losing, is inconsiderate, lacks empathy and rides roughshod over staff, colleagues and competitors alike. They may be financially wealthy and 'successful', but at what cost? The second kind, leaders like Kevin and Mark who you will meet in the case studies in Chapter 9, whilst having all of the positive Director traits of self-confidence, decisiveness, energy, focus, pragmatism, intelligence, rationality and determination, have none of the associated testosterone-driven derailers. Could it be that either they have lower initial baseline levels of testosterone, or that their testosterone is moderated by another biochemical driver, such as serotonin, or even oestrogen? At the moment we don't know the answer, however, it's certainly an interesting theory which would appear to have some substantiating behavioural evidence and support.

In adults, higher testosterone levels correlate with a reduced use of words and language related to social connections and concern for others. Elevated testosterone makes people more self-focused, more egocentric and much less likely to care about any adverse effects to other people[21]. So not only does testosterone make people more motivated, driven, competitive and aggressive, it also makes them less empathetic, less considerate and less concerned about others' well-being: a double whammy. This makes women who have high baseline levels of testosterone particularly easy to identify as they do not match the female, feminine stereotype. Like men, unless they have learnt to moderate their behaviour, they can come across as being competitive and aggressive, selfish and not very likeable. Of course, interestingly, and probably usefully for them, their testosterone protects them from caring very much, if at all.

I know of one female C-suite FTSE 100 executive, who, immediately upon appointment, has every other internal candidate who applied for her role removed from the organization in case they might subsequently threaten her position. She has done this on more than one occasion. It's the corporate jungle equivalent of the male lion, upon becoming the alpha male of the pride, killing all of the pre-adolescent cubs sired by his predecessor.

According to Fisher, there is a negative correlation between testosterone and partner attachment building behaviours. This can manifest itself in the lack of consideration and empathy which some testosterone-driven Transactional Director Leaders pay to their staff and colleagues. Relationships are important to them; however, for those with high baseline testosterone, their overriding question will be "What's in it for me?" Conversely, falling in love and fatherhood decrease men's baseline testosterone levels. Presumably this is an evolutionary device designed to facilitate greater empathy, caring and better communication and listening skills just at those times when they need to communicate most effectively and be more empathetic, nurturing and considerate[22].

Do you remember in Chapter 2 we learned that male leaders are more likely to overrate their performance compared to the ways in which their staff actually perceive them? Could this be an example of the protective effect of testosterone as a confidence enhancer?[23]

Serotonin

Approximately 90% of our serotonin is located within our gastrointestinal tract. However serotonin is also a neurotransmitter. Serotonin appears to be a moderator; it's implicated in the regulation of mood, appetite, sleep and cognitive functions such as memory and learning. It's associated with feelings of well-being, calmness, serenity, faithfulness and loyalty[24], home-building and comfort, both social comfort and physical comfort. It's a mood-balancer. Low levels of serotonin are associated with depression in some people. Carbohydrates such as potatoes and bread trigger the release of serotonin, as do foods such as cakes, which are also high in sugar. This may explain why, in order to comfort themselves when they are feeling low, some people are particularly susceptible to carbohydrate-rich and sugar-laden foods[25].

Interestingly, exercise also raises levels of serotonin in the blood and sunlight helps to synthesise it. The link between outdoor exercise and sunshine lifting depression is anecdotally also well recognised and has led some UK doctors to suggest that getting a dog and walking it every day is one of the best remedial cures for depression that there is. In addition, owning a pet you can stroke is also associated with lower levels of the stress hormone cortisol, and increases in oxytocin, the cuddle hormone.

The Link to Chocolate

Caffeine supresses serotonin. Cocoa raises it. Therefore the higher the cocoa content of chocolate, i.e. the darker it is, the more serotonin is released. Builders, who are driven by serotonin, are often particularly keen on chocolate! In fact, it's one of the questions that I often ask people to quickly identify who might be a Transformational Leader in the room.   Builders don't just like chocolate, they absolutely love it! You may remember I mentioned my architect/builder in the previous chapter. He adores chocolate. For Christmas last year I bought enough bars of it to make up an oblong 'brick'. I wrapped it up in red paper and drew black lines on it so that it looked like a newly built wall. He said that it was one of the best presents he had ever been given.

Serotonin-enhancing anti-depressants can strengthen feelings of attachment within a long-term relationship[26]. Long-term, consistent, stable and sustainable relationships are very much the domain of the Transformational Builder. In fact, Fisher goes so far as to suggest that Builders are the least likely of the four Temperament Types to divorce[27].

If you remember in the Summary Grids in Chapter 3, you may also remember my comment that the grids make it appear that the dopamine-driven Explorer is the behavioural opposite of the serotonin-driven Builder. Elevated serotonin activity can depress the pathways for dopamine[28], potentially making a Builder much less likely to participate in high risk or heightened pleasure activities than the other Temperament Types.

While increasing cortisol, stress depletes serotonin, which suggests that Builders may be particularly susceptible to stress and the effects of it. Physical massage reduces levels of the stress hormone cortisol whilst increasing serotonin and dopamine levels. Reliving happy times and remembering happy memories also boost serotonin levels. These are what I would call protective factors against feeling low or mild depression and are mood enhancers because they boost serotonin levels. All these suggest that perhaps laughter, a walk along the beach or taking the dog out, a good back and shoulder massage, a relaxing hot bath and a drawer full of chocolate could be a great antidote to a stressful life, especially for a Builder.

The Link to Values

I first developed the Thinking Styles™ questionnaire and report in the late 1990s as a way of helping people to understand how their cognitive style preferences influence their leadership and working behaviours. In the years that I've been using it, and following the thousands of feedback sessions that have been delivered, I have come to realise that people's highest preferences, as self-reported in their Thinking Styles™ profiles, fundamentally link to their values. This is true whether someone is predominantly logical, rational and detail conscious, predominantly creative, innovative and strategic, others-focused or driven by complexity, (to name just some of the 26 types of thinking measured by the profiling system).

People will value their primary preferences most highly, over and above all the others. If you don't share their preferences, they will notice. In many ways, that doesn't matter. We all have our own preferences and working styles and if we are intelligent and emotionally mature we don't realistically expect everyone else to be just like us. What is important though – in fact, I would even go so far as to say that it's critical – is that you understand, respect and value the strengths of others' preferred thinking styles. If you don't, they will be offended and your working relationship will be damaged.

I have come to believe that the same is true of the Leadership Temperament Types. We will notice who is like us. We will do this unconsciously, and it's subtle: shared language, similar interests, some kind of intuitive recognition, a feeling of being on the same wavelength ... It's easier to work with people who are just like us; the cognitive, emotional and intellectual effort generates energy rather than stress. We value what they value, and as you know, we are all driven by our values. Conversely, working with, leading or being led by people who are not like us and do not share the same values as us is, quite simply, harder work. That's fine, just so long as three critical words are in place, and they need to be in place from both directions.

These three words are: *understand; respect; and value.*

Now that we've explored some of the supporting biological evidence for the existence of the four Temperament Types, the next chapter gives you the opportunity to learn more about how each of the four Temperament Types think and behave in a managerial or leadership role and to complete some diagnostic questionnaires which will identify your own Leadership Temperament Type preferences.

Chapter 5: Which Type Are You?

Having exploded the myths of the male/female gender stereotypes in Chapters 1 and 2, and introduced you to the theory of Leadership Temperament Types in Chapter 3 with some supporting biological and psychological evidence in Chapter 4, we are probably now at the stage where you really want to know what your own profile is. So this chapter contains two diagnostic questionnaires designed to help you to discover your Leadership Temperament Type drivers. Completing them will enable you to identify your primary and secondary leadership style preferences. In fact, you will be able to generate a score for all four of the Leadership Temperament Types.

Not only will you be able to understand more clearly just what it is which motivates you internally, you will be able to see yourself from the outside, as your team and your colleagues perceive you. This on its own can be a powerful motivator for change and development, should you choose to go down that path. And at the very least, it will increase your self-awareness which, as we will learn later in Chapter 8, is one of the key tenets of Authentic Leadership.

Questionnaire One should be completed twice. The first time, select only **one** response. This will identify your strongest motivational driver and is a direct link to what you **value most**. The second time you complete the questionnaire, tick **all** of the responses which are true for you. This will identify how **flexible** you are in terms of your strategies and behaviours, and is a measure of how **other people** will perceive you.

It's very easy to fool ourselves into thinking that we are somehow different from the way we truly are. In psychological terms, it's called an ego-defence mechanism. You will get the most accurate picture of yourself if you are completely honest when you answer the questions.

Questionnaire One

			1	All
Q1		**How would you describe your general approach?**		
	CE	Enthusiastic	❑	❑
	RN	Kind	❑	❑
	TD	Decisive	❑	❑
	TB	Sensible	❑	❑
Q2		**How would you describe your attitude to life?**		
	CE	Optimistic	❑	❑
	RN	Trusting	❑	❑
	TD	Sceptical	❑	❑
	TB	Realistic	❑	❑
Q3		**What do you worry about?**		
	CE	Being bored	❑	❑
	RN	Being alone	❑	❑
	TD	Being unsuccessful	❑	❑
	TB	Being ostracised	❑	❑
Q4		**Which role would you enjoy?**		
	CE	An Innovator	❑	❑
	RN	A Supporter	❑	❑
	TD	A Decision-maker	❑	❑
	TB	A Defender	❑	❑
Q5		**What is your film preference?**		
	CE	Science fiction or adventure	❑	❑
	RN	Romance or comedy	❑	❑
	TD	Complex thriller or who-dunnit	❑	❑
	TB	Drama or real-life story	❑	❑
Q6		**What do you strive for?**		
	CE	Adventure and excitement	❑	❑
	RN	Intimacy and authenticity	❑	❑
	TD	Knowledge and success	❑	❑
	TB	Social acceptance and harmony	❑	❑

		1	All
Q7	What do you really dislike?		
	CE Repetitive stuff	❏	❏
	RN Unkindness, and/or superficiality	❏	❏
	TD People getting their facts wrong	❏	❏
	TB Unethical actions and/or immorality	❏	❏
Q8	What's important to you?		
	CE Excitement	❏	❏
	RN Collaboration	❏	❏
	TD Influence	❏	❏
	TB Loyalty	❏	❏
Q9	What are you dedicated to?		
	CE Your life and experiences	❏	❏
	RN Relationships and people	❏	❏
	TD Your work and success	❏	❏
	TB Your family and community	❏	❏
Q10	What *don't* you see the relevance of being?		
	CE Compliant	❏	❏
	RN Task focused at the expense of people	❏	❏
	TD Friendly just for the sake of it	❏	❏
	TB Flirtatious	❏	❏
Q11	What are you likely to say?		
	CE *Carpe Diem* – Seize the day!	❏	❏
	RN Are you OK?	❏	❏
	TD What you should do is	❏	❏
	TB Be careful	❏	❏
Q12	What do you feel as if you physically need?		
	CE Excitement, and a degree of risk	❏	❏
	RN Intimacy and authenticity	❏	❏
	TD Intellectual stimulation and to be successful	❏	❏
	TB Familiarity and stability	❏	❏

Your Scores for Questionnaire One

Complete this grid for your first set of scores, when you could only choose one of the options. Take your score, divide it by 12, then multiply by 100 to get a percentage score.

CE		/12 x 100 =	%
RN		/12 x 100 =	%
TD		/12 x 100 =	%
TB		/12 x 100 =	%

Your Values

1st Preference	
2nd Preference	
3rd Preference	
4th Preference	

Complete this grid for your second set of scores, when you could choose all of the options that you feel apply to you. Again, taking your score, dividing it by 12, then multiplying it by 100 will calculate your percentage score.

CE		/12 x 100 =	%
RN		/12 x 100 =	%
TD		/12 x 100 =	%
TB		/12 x 100 =	%

How Others See You

1st Preference	
2nd Preference	
3rd Preference	
4th Preference	

What are these scores showing you? First, where you could only select one option, it's giving you an indication of your **primary drivers** which also link to your **values**. Secondly, when you could choose all of the things which apply to you, it's giving you an indication of how **cognitively and behaviourally flexible** *you are* regarding your strategies and what you actually do in real life. **This will be how other people see you.**

Development Questions for Questionnaire One

- Do you recognise yourself in your scores?

- Did completing Questionnaire One, where you were forced to choose only one answer, give you any insights about yourself? If so, what are they?

- Thinking about the first time you completed Questionnaire One, do you seem to have one predominant Temperament Type or are you balanced across all four?

- Do you have a balance of responses across all four Temperament Types when you could select any and all options? Or did you emerge as having one primary Type?

- Is there a pattern for you between your two sets of scores?

- And whether there is or there isn't, what does this mean for you?

Now let's complete Questionnaire Two and see what that shows us. Questionnaire Two comprises four sets of 25 questions; one set for each Leadership Temperament Type. The types are clustered together rather than randomised for a number of reasons: firstly, it's all part of helping you to become familiar with the model, and secondly, it's not a test! I'm not trying to catch you out here, and clustering the questions together by type makes it easier for you to identify your leadership preferences and flexibilities. Simply tick **all** of the statements which are true for you, (using a yes/no response pattern is the easiest thing to do). Then add up your scores and enter them into the tables at the end of the questionnaire.

This questionnaire is designed to identify your flexibility and will be how **others** see you.

Questionnaire Two
Questions for Transactional Directors

1	People seem to look to me to make decisions	❏
2	I'm comfortable challenging others	❏
3	I would prefer to make a decision for myself than have to abide by someone else's decision	❏
4	I will cut corners if necessary in my drive to get things done	❏
5	I enjoy intellectual debate	❏
6	I find it easy to focus on the task at hand and concentrate until the job's done	❏
7	People who get the facts wrong annoy me	❏
8	I'm forthright in my views and opinions	❏
9	It's critical to think things through logically	❏
10	Failure isn't an option for me	❏
11	I would rather be considered practical than creative	❏
12	I really hate losing	❏
13	I dislike having to put other people first	❏
14	I already have, or would actively seek, a leadership role	❏
15	I dislike ambiguity; I want things to be clear	❏
16	I'm determined to be independent	❏

17	I want my boss's job	❏
18	If someone on my team isn't pulling their weight then they have to go	❏
19	I'm not very emotional	❏
20	I'm pretty tough-minded	❏
21	I'm very competitive and I hate losing	❏
22	I find self-discipline easy; once my mind's made up that's pretty much it	❏
23	The end justifies the means for me	❏
24	I'm driven to win and succeed	❏
25	I sometimes find people too emotional at work	❏

Your total score on the Transactional Director Scale ❏

Questions for Relational Negotiators

1	People are really important to me	❏
2	I always put people before the task if I can	❏
3	People describe me as warm and compassionate	❏
4	I frequently find that colleagues talk to me about their problems	❏
5	I'm highly intuitive	❏
6	Kindness is really important to me	❏
7	I dislike superficial conversations and small talk	❏
8	I would prefer to avoid confrontation and conflict if possible	
9	I often put other people first at work, sometimes against my better judgement	❏
10	I'm comfortable with ambiguity	❏
11	Sometimes I can be too trusting of others	❏
12	I really enjoy meeting new people	❏
13	I always consider everyone's point of view and perspective if I can	❏
14	I sometimes worry about being alone	❏
15	I'm sometimes easily hurt as I can be quite sensitive	❏
16	People say that I'm empathetic	❏
17	I prefer consensus to having to make a decision myself	❏

18	I'm recognised at work for being very supportive of colleagues	❏
19	My role as a manager or leader would be (or is) to nurture my staff	❏
20	I enjoy romantic comedies	❏
21	At work I always try to achieve a win/win situation where everyone's happy	❏
22	I enjoy deep and meaningful conversations with people	❏
23	I've considered counselling, coaching, teaching or training others as a career	❏
24	People tend to share their secrets or personal details of their lives with me	❏
25	I think I would be good at a role involving mediating between people	❏

Your total score on the Relational Negotiator Scale ❏

Questions for Charismatic Explorers

1	'Life is a game, so play it' is my motto	❏
2	If I couldn't have fun at work I would find another job	❏
3	I get very excited by opportunities and possibilities	❏
4	I'm often spontaneous	❏
5	I tend to get restless	❏
6	I hate being bored	❏
7	I would never give up my freedom	❏
8	I find having to wait for things really frustrating	❏
9	I sometimes wish that I had more patience	❏
10	I've been described as impulsive	❏
11	I don't always finish the things that I start	❏
12	Apparently I'm unconventional	❏
13	I will try anything once	❏
14	I have great fun and can be the life and soul of the party	❏
15	Some of my hobbies could be considered to be quite dangerous	❏

16 People find me fun-loving and optimistic ❏
17 I tend to play down risks as I think I can cope with them ❏
18 I tend to have new and innovative ideas ❏
19 When I organise something I often find that people want
     to join me ❏
20 I'm sociable and outgoing ❏
21 I don't really worry about the future ❏
22 I enjoy doing new things ❏
23 I get bored quite easily ❏
24 Freedom to try new things is really important to me ❏
25 I like spontaneity and the unexpected ❏

Your total score on the Charismatic Explorer Scale ❏

Questions for Transformational Builders

1   I'm very patient ❏
2   Family and duty are both very important to me ❏
3   I sometimes find change threatening ❏
4   I prefer not to take unnecessary risks ❏
5   I'm recognised at work for my high ethics ❏
6   Community spirit is important to me ❏
7   I can be quite cautious about things sometimes ❏
8   I like to finish something once I've started it ❏
9   Loyalty is important to me ❏
10 I'm considered to be very reliable by others ❏
11 I love chocolate ❏
12 Family always come first with me ❏
13 Prudence is important ❏
14 I'm always honest ❏
15 Stability is important to me and I dislike things being
     unstable at work ❏
16 I like familiarity; sometimes things that are too new and
     untested make me uncomfortable ❏
17 People describe me as steady, trustworthy and reliable ❏

18	If every day was different and anything could happen I would hate it	❏
19	If something is unethical, I simply won't do it	❏
20	I would fight to change something I thought was unjust	❏
21	I eat bread or potatoes every day	❏
22	I'm pretty cautious and can be quite risk-averse sometimes	❏
23	Dishonesty is something I really dislike	❏
24	I would do a job I hated to provide for my family	❏
25	Fairness is really important to me	❏

Your total score on the Transformational Builder Scale ❏

Your Scores for Questionnaire Two

CE		x 4 =	%
RN		x 4 =	%
TD		x 4 =	%
TB		x 4 =	%

How Others See You

1st Preference	
2nd Preference	
3rd Preference	
4th Preference	

Your Percentage scores for Questionnaire Two

This is simply another way of representing your scores that the highly visual thinkers amongst you will appreciate. Remember, there are no right or wrong answers. The previous grid asks you to take your total score for each Leadership Temperament Type and multiply it by 4 to create a percentage. Now draw your % scores in the bar chart below.

	0%	25%	50%	75%	100%
CE					
RN					
TD					
TB					

N.B. Please be aware that as Questionnaires One and Two are different, your scores for how others see you are unlikely to be **exactly** the same. However, it is likely that your **pattern of responses** will be the same or similar. So, if your scores for **how other's see you** suggest that you're a Director/Builder in Questionnaire One when you can tick all of the responses which you feel are true of you, then you will probably emerge as a Director/Builder in Questionnaire Two as well. If by any chance you don't, then look very carefully at your responses between the two questionnaires and you will probably be able to work out why there is a difference.

Development Questions for Questionnaire Two

- Do you recognise yourself in your scores? They show you as **other people** see you, not necessarily as you see yourself to be.

- Do your scores give you any insights about yourself? If so, what are they?

- Do you seem to have one primary Leadership Temperament Type or are you balanced across all four? A greater balance suggests greater cognitive and behavioural flexibility depending on the situations and circumstances you find yourself in.

- Is there a pattern for you between your two sets of scores over the two questionnaires, and what does this mean for you?

We will be exploring more about what your scores might mean for you and how the four Leadership Temperament Types inter-relate in Chapter 6. Chapter 7 identifies and discusses the dark side of leadership and Chapter 8 introduces you to Authentic Leadership and the three reasons why leaders fail. Chapter 9 consists of ten case studies of real leaders, all Authentic Leaders in their own right, and also includes their scores, which you may find of interest, especially if someone's scores are similar to yours, and particularly if they aren't!

If you want to undertake a more in-depth analysis of your Leadership Temperament Types as they relate to leadership and the world of work, you will find more questionnaire and report options at *www.unitedbychocolate.com* including the word-choice questionnaire used in the case studies.

Chapter 6: Leading, Managing and Influencing

As well as considering the ways in which each Leadership Temperament Type influences, manages and leads others, in this chapter we are going to be discussing the strengths, weaknesses and downsides of each style in a leadership role. I've included the dangers and shortcomings for you so that the picture you get of each Leadership Temperament Type is a complete one, 'warts and all', so to speak. It's important to be able to recognise these downsides so that you understand where they come from if you experience them at work.

Recognising these weaknesses is the first step to being able to manage them, both in yourself and also in those people who display them. Of course, how you deal with them and the person who exhibits them is going to depend on your own Temperament Type, your experience and your personal leadership and management style.

Ideally, everyone would be able to work to their strengths, so it's useful to be able to recognise what these are. In my experience, so often in teams, and at work in general, rather than valuing people's strengths and individual differences, those people who do not share them simply either don't see them or dismiss them if they do, leading to a lack of respect from both sides and subsequently, poor collaboration and compromised organisational results.

This is regrettable, as each of the four Leadership Temperament Types very much has its own strengths which, when harnessed and used appropriately, make teams, departments and organisations significantly stronger, more agile and much more flexible. They are also much nicer places to work in, which translates into lower percentage turnover figures and a future leadership pipeline being grown from within. This is a precious commodity when we consider the practical value of already-established collaborative working relationships, not to mention insider knowledge and the intellectual capital each person possesses.

Charismatic Explorers

Charismatic Explorers are highly creative and innovative and are excellent at strategic, 'blue sky' thinking; 'thinking outside the box'; making connections between related and unrelated things and exploring potential options. They are unconventional, spontaneous, sociable, bold, outgoing and confident. People love to be around them. Explorers enjoy challenge and risk but are not necessarily driven by the desire to win. (That's a Director trait!) However, they do thrive on fast and exciting new projects, and with experience, will also thrive on multiple projects as they relish complexity. They are not afraid of risks and enjoy anything that raises their adrenaline levels. They like to be engaged at work. More than that, they like to be excited by their work and will be passionate about it.

If possible, avoid setting them boundaries and limits which are very tight or strict and allow them to take risks. Remember though that calculated risks are the domain of the Directors, who like to feel in control, so be aware that Charismatic Explorers may take all-or-nothing, win-or-lose, live-or-die kinds of risks, which can make them difficult to lead and manage, and sometimes risky to follow.

As they tend to get bored quickly and will be frustrated by any lack of progress, you will need to find ways to keep them interested. This means that they are often keen on learning new things and will thrive in an environment where they can either focus on one specific project or, with a broader remit, explore ways to be creative and innovative, treading paths as yet undiscovered.

Charismatic Explorers are extremely upbeat, positive, fun to be around and optimistic. The words 'no' and 'can't' are not in their vocabulary. Use them for breaking the rules, engaging and exciting followers, being innovative and taking appropriate, 'creative' risks.

The Weaknesses of the Charismatic Explorer

- Other people may follow them because they are charismatic and exciting to be around; however, very often they're not really interested in actually having a leadership role or responsibility for others as they just want to do their own thing and tread their own path.

- Noradrenaline and dopamine activation means that the Charismatic Explorer is likely to downplay risks and risk factors. That's if they see them and recognise them as risky and potentially dangerous in the first place – they may not.

- The same chemical biology also means that it's quite possible, even quite likely, that they will take greater risks than the other Leadership Temperament Types. It's this that often helps them to be 'entrepreneurial'. However, it can also mean that they may sometimes have flexible or questionable ethics.

- They are easily bored and may lack patience. They may also lack self-awareness, self-regulation and discipline.

- If they don't achieve their desired results quickly enough, they are likely to move on to the next thing, which means that they won't always finish or complete the tasks and projects that they begin.

- They can often be impulsive and may jump in 'too early' before a project is properly thought through or before the risk assessments have been done.

- Their restlessness and need for excitement means that they are attracted to danger, which can mean that they may also put other people in danger or expose them to risks. These risks might not be physical as such, but may involve someone potentially losing their job if a risky plan or investment doesn't pay off.

- Because the Charismatic Explorer thrives on excitement, if it doesn't exist naturally in their lives, either personally or professionally, they will create it.

- They can have a short attention span and are easily distracted.

- The Charismatic Explorer really hates their freedom to do things being restricted and so they may bend or even break the rules to get around things and achieve their aims. This is because, at the extreme, they are solely driven by their own agenda.

- They will leave behind those people who can't keep up with them, or those who try to slow them down or curb their enthusiasm and freedom.

- Chraismatic Explorers don't like to feel over-managed, controlled or badly led.   Even if they are in a job role they enjoy, ultimately they will leave if their own personal and professional needs aren't being met. Where the Builder will do a job which they hate in order to provide for their family, in contrast, the Explorer will simply walk away, positive in their belief that something better is just around the corner.

Relational Negotiators

First and foremost, if you want to influence a Negotiator, be their friend. They are highly motivated by the quality of relationships and their friendships are very, very important to them. Share personal insights with them and let them know what's important to you and what makes you tick. There is a caveat here: Directors are often very secretive; they have a fear that someone who has information about them will use it to manipulate them to their own ends. Of course, the Negotiator would not do this; however, another Director might, and as they frequently think that everyone else is just like them, they play their cards very close to their chests and are often difficult to get to know. Interestingly, of the people who agreed to be interviewed as case studies for the book and who then dropped out or were suddenly unavailable, all, I would predict, were Directors! However, because Relational Negotiators are so genuine and understanding, they will happily accept the Director for whom they are without probing too far or taking advantage in any way.

This is perhaps one of the reasons why Negotiators and Directors often form such close working relationships: a Negotiator is non-competitive and will be a trusted aide. They will support the Director, balancing and mediating the Director's lack of people-oriented, 'soft' skills. Interestingly, Fisher suggests that within a romantic partnership, Negotiators and Directors often marry. What she doesn't tell us, however, is how many of these partnerships end in divorce when there is the inevitable clash of values down the line! I suspect that there will also be many close working relationships that ultimately share the same fate.

Relational Negotiators are people focused and pro-social from a person-oriented, rather than a community, perspective. This means that they are more concerned with an individual's well-being and the impact of actions on them than they will be about the impact on society as a whole. It also means that in the Boardroom they will argue for the needs and rights of the individual and will want to understand the impact that decisions have on groups of people. If you want to understand the employees' perspective, ask a Negotiator. From a multiple stakeholder approach, they want to consider the impact and consequences on everyone, and they will value everyone equally. It's this characteristic of equality of caring above all others which makes the relational Negotiator so good in areas such as training and development, mediation and human resources.

When working with a Negotiator, be kind. Be caring. Be inclusive. Be sensitive. Ask them how they feel about issues and remember that they will appreciate your being as flexible as they are. If you need to negotiate with them, do it in ways which are win/win rather than win/lose.

Be aware that the Negotiator's flexibility, kindness and compassion should not be perceived as weakness. Potentially, initially, because they often dislike confrontation and aggressive behaviour, other Leadership Temperament Types, most notably the Director, may attempt to, and will often succeed in, bullying the Negotiator into submission. By this I mean they make the Negotiator accept certain decisions or courses of action which, actually, they don't really agree with. This will only be a short-term situation. I have seen this many, many times in both business and commerce and also within the voluntary sector. Ultimately, the Negotiator has a core of steel and they will walk away from any relationship which doesn't work for them. The Director will have lost an ally and a valuable supporter, and in the long term as well as over the shorter term, the organisation will be diminished and the employees will mourn their loss.

The Weaknesses of the Relational Negotiator

- They may find decision-making difficult if there's no way of being able to keep everyone happy. This is particularly true if very difficult decisions have to be made which will affect people's well-being, such as downsizing or redundancy.

- They can be over-sensitive and easily hurt, often taking criticism to heart.

- It's possible that they may avoid confrontation and not be 'brave' enough to challenge others, even if it's necessary.

- Directors in particular may perceive them as being 'too soft'.

- They may lack the ambition or drive to take the lead and are often happy to take a supporting role.

- It can sometimes take them a long time to recover from setbacks as they may be very affected by disagreements, often carrying emotional episodes around with them for some time.

- As people and relationships are more important to them than tasks, sometimes the completion of tasks or projects may be delayed or overlooked as people are put first.

- Agreed targets, goals or results may not be achieved.

- They can become over-emotional.

- Because they always consider the multiple stakeholder perspective they may have a slower decision-making style compared to some of the other Leadership Temperament Types.

- Potentially, as they care so much about the well-being of others, the Relational Negotiator can be easily manipulated and taken advantage of by less caring and more ruthless colleagues or staff with a plausible 'sob story'.

- This explains why they often put others first to the detriment of themselves and sometimes, their physical or emotional well-being.

- They are likely to be high on self-awareness; however, they may over-share personal information and they can sometimes imagine that they know what people are thinking and feeling without the supporting evidence to back their theories up.

- They are often idealistic, and therefore may be perceived by some of their more pragmatic and realistic colleagues as being 'unrealistic'.

- They can become highly introspective, almost obsessive, and may on occasion develop unhealthy, co-dependent relationships.

- They may become frustrated and resentful if they feel that they 'have' to help others and put others first. This can mean that they become passive/aggressive towards those people they are expected to support and nurture.

- They can be determined to help you, whether you want their assistance or not!

Transactional Directors

Directors like facts and evidence, so if you work for one, be prepared to be asked for those. It's actually better to present them early to support your position. Be on time, not late; Directors hate being kept waiting or having their time wasted. Be logical, not emotional; Directors dislike displays of emotion. They don't feel uncomfortable about them, simply unmoved. They are pointless and display weakness, according to the way a Transactional Director sees the world. If you get it wrong, apologise and don't try to justify your position or your actions. Especially don't try to apportion blame or say anything emotional or unprofessional; instead, focus on how to resolve the issue quickly and with the minimum of fuss.

Don't try to be their friend. Focus on the tasks at hand and on what needs to be achieved instead. Don't waffle. Be results-oriented and make sure that you deliver on time. Do what you say that you are going to do. You must always deliver. If you don't they will notice, they will remember, and they will hold it against you in the future. Don't bother to share personal information with them; they simply aren't interested. Always be specific, avoiding any ambiguity, as Directors like clarity. They also like certainty as it enables them to be more confident. Transactional Directors always come across as being confident; it's one of the positive personality effects of testosterone.

Don't drop in on a Director unannounced; they won't appreciate it and it's unlikely that they will have the time to see you as they are always busy, active people. The same goes for a phone call to 'catch up'. Whilst the Negotiator would appreciate that, the Director simply won't see the point of it. If you want to see them or speak with them, book an appointment and a specific time in their schedule, while being clear about the purpose of the meeting and any outcomes you may have.

It's important to respond to the Director's desire for debate. They do like to talk about things, but be prepared for them to be direct and directive. They relish intellectual challenge remember, but don't take any of their comments personally as they probably won't realise when they are being insensitive. You can challenge them back quite hard, but avoid getting personal with them as they can have fragile egos, which means that they bruise easily and are likely to lash out at you or even strike pre-emptively if they feel threatened in any way.

The Weaknesses of the Transactional Director

- They can be very, very competitive and they hate losing, which can make them difficult to work with at times, especially if they are competing against you.

- They can be over-controlling, insensitive to others and are sometimes accused of bullying behaviours.

- They can be prone to angry outbursts and emotional flooding, especially if they lose or if things don't go their way.

- They can lack both self-awareness and self-regulation. They lack empathy and always bear a grudge.

- In their drive to win, (or not lose), they may sometimes make unethical decisions, cut corners, and ignore or overlook the implications and consequences of their decisions for real people.

- They can be either emotionally detached and disengaged or so passionate and engaged about something that they come across as aggressive.

- Because they really dislike ambiguity, (as it makes them feel insecure and therefore uncomfortable), they may sometimes rush decision-making, or push through decisions or actions without thinking things through carefully enough.

- They can be intellectual snobs who dismiss those they don't consider as bright as they are. They can bully anyone they don't respect, especially as they can be prone to challenging everyone and everything.

- Because they need certainty and evidence, Directors can come across as sceptical, untrusting and over-demanding of proof. Their constant insistence on the verification that coaching works and their constant demand for the supporting evidence for the so-called 'soft skills' which they themselves so desperately need, is something which I, as an Executive Coach find extremely wearing. Even when they are presented with the supporting evidence for people-skills being good for business - they frequently dismiss it! I have come to believe that this is because they simply don't 'get' the value of soft skills. They are soft-skills blind as well as mind-blind, and as supporting evidence for that possibly controversial statement I'm going to cite Baron-Cohen's work on autism and the extreme male brain!

- They can become obsessed with power, rank and command and may, if unchecked, end up suffering from Hubris Syndrome, which we will go on to explore in Chapter 7.

- They can be impatient and often hate being told what to do. They may sabotage change initiatives that are not their idea and in order to save face will often try to hide their losses and failures.

- If they are not in a position of power, or if they don't feel in control, they can be disruptive, and they may be unwilling to help others unless there's something in it for them.

- If they are women, Transactional Directors can become particularly aggressive, (remember the gender stereotyping in Chapter 2), and they often lack the self-awareness to realise just how difficult they can be to be around.

- Higher baseline levels of testosterone mean that they can be arrogant, they can be unethical and they can be selfish.

- They can be so forthright and direct that they upset people and appear rude and anti-social. As they often miss the emotional and linguistic clues as to how the other people around them are feeling, they can come across as boorish and unpleasant to be with.

Transformational Builders

Transformational Builders want to create and build long-term, sustainable partnerships, both with people and with organisations. They are driven by loyalty and are absolutely committed to people and causes. Solid, mature and responsible citizens in their thinking even from a young age, they can find any changes which they feel are imposed on them very threatening, so be cautious with them and suggest gradual, not radical, change. Builders will always prefer a traditional, tried and tested approach that will lead to long-term, sustainable change in projects which will endure over time for the greater good.

As Transformational Builders are the most pro-social of all of the four Leadership Temperament Types, make the effort to clearly identify how their work contributes to their organisation, community or to society in general. If you can, ask for their input or support on community or social projects; not only will they really enjoy these, they will form strong bonds with colleagues and you can rely on them to make the project work over both the short and longer-terms. You must be ethical in all that you do however, so don't try to cut corners. When it comes to risk-taking, avoid unnecessary risks and be aware that even suggesting a slightly risky course of action is unlikely to be received well and may make them feel uncomfortable.

It has occurred to me as I'm writing these paragraphs that just as there may be a predominance of Transactional Director Types working in business and commerce, where the focus is on success, profit and winning, there may be a predominance of Builder Types working within the UK civil service and the local government public sector. As Builders are cautious, even risk-averse, committed, loyal, ethical and incorruptible, hard-working and neither focused on profit nor on winning, this makes complete sense. It's only a working theory of course; however, it does seem to make intuitive sense, especially when I consider my own stepfather, who did a job in local government that he hated for 40 years in order to provide for his extended family.

Ask a Transformational Builder to work with you; remember that they are highly collaborative. Avoid being inconsistent with them and changing your mind. Always tell the truth, not your version of it; they really hate white lies or strategic omissions of information and if you do that they will never trust you again. They are moderate and cautious in all that they do, so avoid extremes, over-reacting or becoming too passionate as this can make them feel uncomfortable. If possible, build in reflection time to decision-making so that they have the time to consider things without feeling railroaded by time pressures.

Transformational Builders make excellent committee members and Chairs. They are inclusive, fair, open, honest, collaborative, solid, trustworthy and completely reliable. They are never going to set the world on fire, (the Explorers will do that); however, at their best they are great team players who will create something worthwhile and lasting within existing and expected social norms.

The Weaknesses of the Transformational Builder

- They may write off other people who don't share their high ethical standards, and they can come across as stubborn, inflexible, over-cautious and extremely risk-averse.

- They will dislike change if they feel that it's being done to them, rather than involving them in the decision-making and implementation process. If they feel that the pace of change is too fast or the changes being made are either untested or too radical, they will become nervous. In this sense, they will become the brakes of a project, or in the worst case, they can kill off a project completely by putting barriers and obstacles in its way.

- Because they will often be the social pillars of their community, they can become obsessed with their reputation and social standing.

- They can be dogmatic in their beliefs about what's right and wrong, and about the 'right' way of doing something. This means

71

they can become what's known as a 'jobsworth'; having an over-reliance on rules, regulations and compliance, becoming inflexible and sometimes difficult to work with.

- They can be over-moralistic and judgemental of others and the ways in which other people choose to live their lives.

- Elevated serotonin levels can reduce creativity so don't expect them to be innovative or exciting in any way; that's the role of the Explorer.

- In order to cope with the stresses and strains of modern living, they may 'self-medicate' with bread, potatoes, and chocolate, as all of these encourage serotonin production. This is especially true of female Builders; it seems that male Builders will sometimes self-medicate with exercise instead, (possibly as they then feel less guilty about eating chocolate!).

Now that we've explored the strengths and weaknesses of each Leadership Temperament Type and you have a good idea how to lead, manage, work with and influence each type, let's consider the dark side of leadership and those leadership derailers which I alluded to in Chapter 2. These build on the potential weaknesses of each type which we have learned about in this chapter. You will undoubtedly recognise some, if not all, of the characteristics.

Chapter 7: The Dark Side of Leadership

I would like to introduce you to the 'dark side' of Leadership. This isn't a veiled reference to anything from *Star Wars*, but rather to the characteristics, factors and traits which, if left unchecked, can lead to leadership derailment. The ideas which I'm going to share with you here aren't my research, however they are all academically published research, and should you want to learn more about any of them or go into more depth, they are all easily found on the internet.

Hogan and Hogan[1] identified 10 dysfunctional dispositions which, at the extreme, even if they are not used very often, can cause management and leadership failure. These personality traits become derailers when the positive elements of them become over-used and the manager or leader lacks the flexibility to adapt their thinking and behaviours appropriately.

As I describe them here I wonder whether you can identify which of the four Leadership Temperament Types would be most likely to display them:

1. **Excitability.** These people lack emotional stability and tend to erupt into emotional displays of shouting, throwing things, slamming doors, bullying, general aggression and other tantrum-type behaviours.

2. **Argumentative.** These people are unwilling to compromise; they will argue vehemently for their position, challenging others aggressively. They are often low on trust and are hyper-vigilant for signs of betrayal. They absolutely refuse to back down or compromise in any way.

3. **Caution.** These people feel threatened by change. They hate novelty and untested ideas. They are very concerned about what others think of them and are fearful of being criticised. They are both indecisive and over-controlling.

4. **Detachment.** These people are completely self-absorbed. They lack social insights and are completely indifferent to either criticism or social warmth from others. They are insensitive and very poor at communicating.

5. **Leisurely.** These people insist on working at their own pace. They often pretend to be hard-working and co-operative and can be very sensitive to disrespect. They can be retaliatory and vengeful, but only under conditions of high deniability where they won't be exposed.

6. **Arrogance.** These people have very high self-esteem and a sense of entitlement. They have exaggerated expectations and are over-confident of success. They will take all the credit for any successes but will deny any responsibility for failure, often blaming others.

7. **Mischievous.** These people think of others as utilities to be exploited and are confident but unpredictable. They fail to deliver on commitments and violate others' expectations of them. They are manipulative, untruthful and untrustworthy.

8. **Imaginative.** These people are eccentric and often, frankly, just odd. They are highly changeable, and can be both self-absorbed and insensitive.

9. **Diligence.** These people are overly rule-bound. They are unable to prioritise and are very poor in a crisis. They are obsequious to authoritarian figures, and make over-fussy, nit-picking micro-managers who over-control people, processes and standards.

10. **Dutiful.** These people are very poor decision-makers. They are unsupportive of staff, and won't challenge authority. They lack courage.

---

[1] Adapted from: Hogan, R. and Hogan, J., (2001). Assessing Leadership: A View from the Dark Side. International Journal of Selection and Assessment, Vol. 9, (1–2), pp.40–51.

To make it more interesting for you, rather than simply giving you the answers here of what I consider to be the most likely Leadership Temperament Type or Types to display each of these poor behaviours, you will find my suggestions at the end of the chapter.

Other researchers have argued that derailed leaders are essentially deficient in one or more of four key areas of competence[2]. Interestingly, two of these areas are personal ones while the other two are professional ones.   They are:

*   **Intrapersonal skills** – self-awareness and empathy

*   **Interpersonal skills** – social skills and emotional intelligence

*   **Business skills** – planning, organising and monitoring

*   **Leadership skills** – team building and role modeling

The same researchers have also identified five 'early warning signs' of management and leadership failure which in theory could apply to any of the four Leadership Temperament Types, but in practice, and you may be recognising a pattern here, will probably be more prevalent in some of the Types than in others:

1. **Poor Results** – such as customer complaints; cover-ups; inaccurate or misleading financial reporting and missed objectives.

2. **Narrow Perspectives** – for example, being out of date; too reliant on technical skills or being too detail-focused.

3. **Poor Team Building** – including such things as autocratic decision-making, micro-management, a lack of training and development and a subsequent high turnover of staff.

4. **Poor Working Relationships** – due to insensitivity, being abrasive or abusive.

5. **Inappropriate or Immature Behaviours** – for example, gossiping, being poor at coping or a refusal to accept responsibility.

[3] Adapted from: Hogan, R., Hogan, J. and Kaiser, R., (2009). Management Derailment. In S. Zedeck, (ed.) American Psychological Association Handbook of Industrial and Organizational Psychology. NY: APA.

I would now like to introduce you to Hubris Syndrome. Hubris is fundamentally linked to power and arrogance. Any of the four Leadership Temperament Types can potentially become susceptible to hubristic behaviours, although because there is a direct link between power and testosterone, it is most likely to affect Transactional Directors; especially those who stop listening to their trusted advisors who, as we discussed earlier, are often likely to be Relational Negotiators or Transformational Builders and who can, when things work well, mediate and moderate the decision-making and approach of the Director.

Dr. David Owen was a medically qualified practitioner before entering British politics, where he eventually rose to become Foreign Secretary in James Callaghan's government. He has written at length about how power perverts decency and the effects that power has on Heads of State, physically, emotionally, behaviourally and cognitively. His book *The Hubris Syndrome: Bush, Blair and the Intoxication of Power* is a fascinating insight into how power can corrupt, and how absolute power can corrupt absolutely. He is one of the Founders of The Daedalus Trust. A UK organisation dedicated to understanding and sharing information about how power can distort decision-making and create personality changes in our modern leaders.

Hubris, like Baron-Cohen's autism, goes beyond Leadership Temperament Types. Yet we can see within Hubris Syndrome how high baseline testosterone and a pre-disposition for Transactional Director Leadership, with its inherent lack of compassion and empathy for others, and its lack of self-awareness, could fuel the embers of a fire that has already been lit by the taste of power within our leaders of today, and arguably, with hindsight, may have driven many historical leadership figures.

This is how I think that the 10 management and leadership derailers are likely to relate to the Leadership Temperament Types. Remember though that these are only my thoughts based on my experience, and that there is, at the moment, no researched evidence to statistically support these predictions.

1. **Excitability.** *These people lack emotional stability and tend to erupt into emotional displays of shouting, throwing things, slamming doors, bullying, general aggression and other tantrum type behaviours.* I think that this is most likely to describe the Transactional Director, although potentially, the Charismatic Explorer might also display some of these traits.

2. **Argumentative.** *These people are unwilling to compromise; they will argue vehemently for their position, challenging others aggressively. They are often low on trust and are hyper-vigilant for signs of betrayal. They absolutely refuse to back down or compromise in any way.* These behaviours would be most likely to be displayed by the Transactional Director.

3. **Cautiousness.** *These people are threatened by change. They hate novelty and untested ideas. They are very concerned about what others think of them and are fearful of being criticised.* They are both indecisive and over-controlling. The Transformational Builder springs to mind for me here.

4. **Detachment.** *These people are completely self-absorbed. They lack social insights and are completely indifferent to either criticism from others or social warmth.* They are insensitive and very poor at communicating. Again, the Transactional Director would be my first choice here due to the testosterone and poor communication link. However, there may also be a potential link to Baron-Cohen's autistic spectrum and so we may also for example find some high-functioning academics or research scientists displaying some of these traits. These may have Explorer as their predominant temperament type, although we

couldn't describe them as personally charismatic as such. They would be 'introverted Explorers' rather than the more usual extroverted types

5. **Leisurely.** *These people insist on working at their own pace. They often pretend to be hard-working and co-operative and can be very sensitive to disrespect. They are retaliatory and vengeful but only under conditions of high deniability where they won't be exposed.* These are difficult to pin down. My first thought is that these could be Charismatic Explorer characteristics; however, they could also fit with the Transactional Director and even with the Transformational Builder.

6. **Arrogance.** *These people have very high self-esteem and a sense of entitlement. They have exaggerated expectations and are over-confident of success. They will take all the credit for any successes but will deny any responsibility for failure, often blaming others.* Once again, because of the potential link to high baseline testosterone and the over-confidence it can give, these seem most likely to be Transactional Director traits, although they may also apply to a Charismatic Explorer.

7. **Mischievous.** *These people think of others as utilities to be exploited and are confident but unpredictable. They fail to deliver on commitments and violate others' expectations of them. They are manipulative, untruthful and untrustworthy.* Most likely to be an Charismatic Explorer.

8. **Imaginative.** *These people are eccentric and often, frankly, just odd. They are highly changeable, and are both self-absorbed and insensitive.* Again, these characteristics are most likely, I think, to be exhibited by the Charismatic Explorer.

9. **Diligence.** *These people are overly rule-bound. They are unable to prioritise and are very poor in a crisis. They are obsequious to authoritarian figures, and make over-fussy, nit-picking micro-managers who over-control people, processes and standards.*

These descriptive traits have the weaknesses of the Transformational Builder written all over them!

10. **Dutiful.** *These people are very poor decision-makers. They are unsupportive of staff, and won't challenge authority. They lack courage.* Once again, these characteristics are, I think, most likely to be those of the Transformational Builder.

[1] Adapted from: Hogan, R. and Hogan, J. (2001), Assessing Leadership: A View from the Dark Side. International Journal of Selection and Assessment, Vol. 9, (1–2), pp. 40–51.

One of the most interesting things here, for me at least, is the complete absence of leadership derailers from the perspective of the Relational Negotiator, who, in fairness, does have their weaknesses! Remember that I didn't identify these derailer traits; these come from other, independent, highly respected academic researchers with whom I have no connection. Could this apparent lack of significant people-oriented weaknesses from the Relational Negotiator explain why there is an increasingly loud call for more sensitive, nurturing, caring, collaborative and possibly 'feminine' leadership style behaviours, not just in the Boardroom but in all organisations and at all levels? Referring back to some of the research we read about in Chapter 2, does UK leadership style perhaps need to become less stereotypically gendered and more 'European'?

Is there such a thing as the perfect leader? I suspect not. However, as well as the call for a gentler, less aggressive approach within business and politics, there also seems to be a desire for more 'authentic leadership' as modern society objects to the manipulation, lies and scandals which so often nowadays seem to beset business, politics, public media figures, celebrity sports people and those people we are meant to admire and look up to. But what actually is Authentic Leadership and why do we assume that it will be somehow better than what we already have? Chapter 8 explains why this is. The 3 Pillars model of Authentic Leadership which you will find within Chapter 8 emerged from my original doctoral research with UK business leaders and senior officers from the UK's Royal Air Force.

Chapter 8: Authentic Leadership and the 3 Reasons Why Leaders Fail

The poor quality thinking, lack of self-control and the aggressive and manipulative behaviours which I described as leadership derailers in the previous chapter ultimately lead to a lack of trust in someone and a lack of respect for them as a role model, whether they are a leader, a manager or simply a co-worker and colleague. It seems that trust within working relationships is important. In fact, it seems that trust is more than important; it's critical.

In 2009, a Gallup research team asked more than 10,000 followers what they wanted from their leaders. The answers will not surprise some of you, especially if you are a Leadership Temperament Type that is either that of the Relational Negotiator, or the Transformational Builder. However, if you are a Transactional Director, or even a Charismatic Explorer, what your followers want may have escaped your attention. The Gallup research identified that the four things followers want from their leaders are not task-focused or results-driven. They are neither operational nor strategic, and they say less about what a leader *does* than who a leader *is* in terms of their personal characteristics and values.

In priority order, the first thing that followers want most from their leaders is to be able to trust them, to believe in them and to believe that what they say is true. The second thing that followers say that they want, and remember that *ten thousand* followers were asked, is that they want a leader to be compassionate, to have empathy and to genuinely care about their well-being. Thirdly, followers want stability, which is something that many leaders either overlook as unimportant, or simply don't seem to realise, in their relentless drive for change, performance improvements and financial savings, is lacking. Finally, followers want to feel hopeful about the future, something that is impossible without trust first being present.

In order to be trusted, it is not enough for a leader simply to view themselves as being ethical in all their dealings. They have to be seen by their colleagues, their followers and the broader community as being principled and honest, competent and fair. With modern social media and the focus on transparency and ethics, more than ever before organisations and the leaders within them are having their values and behaviours examined under a microscope. Many are found wanting.

When I began researching the area of authentic leadership in the very early days of my PhD, I was often frustrated by the fact that every writer on the subject seemed to include different characteristics in their own conceptualisation of the term, most often without any researched evidence to support their claims. It was after all, at that time, simply a theory. There was considerable overlap in the literature and the subject was fragmented and confused at best. There was an American model which purported to show the components of Authentic Leadership; however, intuitively, it didn't seem quite right to me, and it has since been heavily criticised by some academic researchers for certain statistical anomalies which fundamentally call its findings into question. It also used students with very little or no leadership experience as its population sample, not something which, as a practitioner, I would ever do. I wondered whether Authentic Leadership might turn out to be slightly different in the UK, especially if we were to use real leaders to explore and investigate it.

I made the bold statement earlier that being *authentic* as a leader is not the same as being an *Authentic Leader*. This can take a while to get your head around. What I mean is that being *authentic*, (small a, used as an adjective), is not the same thing as being an *Authentic Leader*, (capital A, capital L, the two words used as a noun). It transpires that being an Authentic Leader involves a specific set of behaviours and characteristics, but until I did my research using real business leaders in the UK and senior serving UK military leaders from the Royal Air Force, no one actually knew what they were. My doctoral research simplified and streamlined the complexities of Authentic

Leadership, so now we do know what these behaviours and characteristics are and I can share the results of my research with you here.

When I speak with organisations and at conferences about Authentic Leadership, I call it *The Courage to Lead*. To understand why I do that we need to consider the definition and origin of the word *courage* as its meaning and use has altered significantly over the years.

Courage ... from old French *cuer* meaning heart

- The quality of mind and spirit that enables a person to face danger with bravery
- (Obsolete) The heart as the source of emotion. Compassion, empathy
- Acting in accordance with one's beliefs and values in the face of criticism or danger

---

So courage used to mean having a heart, being moved to compassion and sharing an empathy for others. However, that usage of the word is obsolete today and we are now more familiar with courage being used to denote bravery: both physical and emotional. My preference is to use the definitions of both bravery and compassion, so that when we think about Authentic Leadership and Authentic Leaders, we think of them as possessing both physical and emotional bravery as well as compassion.

Authentic Leadership links who you are as a person, your beliefs and values, with how you lead and manage, your personality, your thinking and your behaviours. To be authentic is to be true to your own ethical standards of conduct, to live a life where what you say and do match so that you have congruence, and importantly, are also consistent with what you believe, your principles and how you feel. Personal authenticity, however, as we already know from the dark side of leadership and the weaknesses of each of the Leadership Temperament Types, can be egocentric and self-serving. We could argue that every dictator and hubristic leader is being personally authentic to themselves. Therefore, being an Authentic Leader involves much more than simply being true to yourself, as we will go on to examine later on in the chapter.

Another useful framework is to think of the ABC of Authentic Leadership as being:
- A for Authenticity: being true to yourself and to your values
- B for Bravery: having the courage to lead and to do the right thing, especially in the face of danger or dissent
- C for Compassion: leading with empathy and a concern for the physical and emotional well-being of others.

Authenticity can be described as consistency and congruence between someone's beliefs and values and their behaviour: 'walking the talk', in other words. While an antique piece of furniture can be described as being either real or fake, authentic or not authentic, when we are talking about people, from a psychological perspective, authenticity is not considered to be an either/or condition; rather, people are best described as being more or less authentic or inauthentic. So why is there such a desire for authenticity?

Research suggests that the individual benefits of leading an authentic life include: increased self-confidence, a greater general feeling of being successful at work and in life, better quality relationships and greater feelings of happiness and well-being, combined with decreased stress, anxiety and illness. Overall, being authentic at work and leading an authentic life can be said to engender greater health and even, some research suggests, a longer life[2]. Why wouldn't everyone want that?

I think the answer to this very big philosophical question is that while everyone would want to live a longer, happier and more authentic and fulfilled life, it's very hard sometimes to have the personal or professional courage to live one's life completely authentically.

Sometimes we don't actually know what we want or need. Sometimes we don't feel brave enough, or sometimes, what we may want personally could hurt those around us, and so we muddle through somehow, trying to do the best we can and to be the best we can, ever hopeful that one day we will get there, wherever 'there' is for us.

Organisationally, apart from growing more effective leaders from within and better team working, the benefits of Authentic Leadership include: increased employee engagement, greater creativity and more effective problem-solving, an increased sense of employee well-being, lower absence and sickness rates and decreased employee turnover[2]. At every level then, individually, organisationally and at the follower and team levels, Authentic Leadership makes sense.

So what's the difference between personal authenticity as a leader and being an Authentic Leader? What is it that Authentic Leaders are perceived to be doing by their followers which leaders who are simply being authentic and true to themselves aren't doing?

When I carried out the literature review I read everything that I could find on the subject of Authentic Leadership. I came across hundreds or articles and an array of different cognitive and behavioural characteristics. Interestingly, I found that they weren't contradictory. They were all positive traits. It was just that there were so many of them, and many of them were very similar! So a major part of my PhD research became about simplifying the concept and construct of Authentic Leadership so that it becomes much easier for people to understand. In academia it's known as the 'relevance/rigour' debate. I believe that you need both.

There is a caveat here. Being an Authentic Leader isn't for the faint-hearted. It really does take courage in every sense of the word. Being an Authentic Leader means much more than simply being yourself. It means being your *best self* and being a *role model* to others, always. That's 24/7, 365 days a year, not just when it suits you. Authentic Leadership is a *way of being* as much as it is a way of living your life and 'doing' leadership, and as we've already identified from the weaknesses of the Leadership Temperament Types and the dark side of leadership, not everyone is capable of being or becoming an Authentic Leader; the standards of self-awareness, discipline and ethics it requires are simply too high for many people to achieve.

But before I put you off aspiring to Authentic Leadership, let's have a look at what it actually is. I won't bore you with the statistical research methodologies I needed to use in my PhD research to be able to identify, with a high degree of certainty, what Authentic Leadership is made up of. As I said earlier, I was lucky enough to be able to work with real UK leaders, from both business and the military, as the population samples for my research, with each group having an average length of leadership experience of approximately 20 years. By using genuine leaders with actual leadership experience, and by replicating the results over two completely different population samples, which included both men and women, we can be confident that the model of Authentic Leadership which emerged from the research is robust, real and relevant.

The 3 Pillars of Authentic Leadership model which emerged from the research is shared with you in Diagram 3 and is shown as a Greek temple. This is quite deliberate as it suggests the link between Authentic Leadership and Aristotelian Virtue Ethics, where a virtuous person is someone who possesses what Aristotle considered to be ideal character traits.

The 3 Pillars of Authentic Leadership comprises the three factors of Self-Awareness, Self-Regulation and Ethics. As you will see in Diagram 3, these are conceptualised as sheltering under the roof of relationships and resting on the bedrock of trust.

I should add that the behaviours and traits which sit within each pillar are only representative. There's more going on as we will discover.

The 3 Pillars of Authentic Leadership

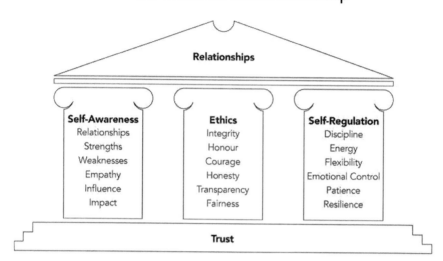

Self-Awareness	Ethics	Self-Regulation
Relationships	Integrity	Discipline
Strengths	Honour	Energy
Weaknesses	Courage	Flexibility
Empathy	Honesty	Emotional Control
Influence	Transparency	Patience
Impact	Fairness	Resilience

Trust

Self-Awareness

The first pillar is Self-Awareness. It includes, but of course is not limited to, things like: knowing your real strengths and weaknesses, understanding how other people perceive you, knowing when and how to be empathetic towards others and being acutely aware of how your thoughts and emotions influence your language and behaviours and, therefore, the impact and influence that you have on others. It is the ability to articulate your core beliefs and values, and understand your personal boundaries and emotional and intellectual drivers. In short, it's knowing who you are and what you value, thereby building a secure sense of your true self, providing an anchor for your decision-making and actions. It is mindfulness. We become self-aware in relation to our interactions and our dealings with other people. Therefore Self-Awareness also includes, by default, Other-Awareness; that is, the Theory of Mind, (if you remember the diagram in Chapter 1 on Baron-Cohen's work), which means the ability to predict, accurately, what other people might be thinking and feeling and therefore the effect that we might have on them. Developing self-awareness is not a one-off; it's a lifelong journey and its lessons are not always comfortable ones.

Self-Regulation

Self-Regulation is closely connected with how well you know and understand yourself. It concerns self-management: your focus, your self-discipline, your ability to be actively and deliberately in control of your thoughts, emotions, your language and behaviours, your levels of tolerance and patience, how you manage your energy, the degree to which you remain approachable when under pressure, how you use humour, your physical, mental and emotional resilience and your cognitive, behavioural and emotional flexibility. In my research, being considered to be a role model by others was most closely related to this pillar of Authentic Leadership.

Ethics

Sitting neatly within the Ethical pillar of Authentic Leadership is professional integrity: your ethical decision-making. Those core beliefs and values which underpin your personal leadership philosophy, the courage to remain steadfast in the face of ethical dissent or wrongdoing by others, having a pro-social leadership ethos, and the desire to serve the wider community. There is also honesty, openness, trust, transparency, fairness, the ethical capacity to be able to judge dilemmas from multiple perspectives, and being able to take into consideration different stakeholder needs.

One of the weaknesses of the whole field of Authentic Leadership, indeed of any of the leadership philosophies which include an ethical component in their make-up, is the thorny question of *whose ethics?* One person's ethical acceptability will be another's ethical dilemma. There is no easy answer to this except to say that over many years I have come to believe that anything that could potentially cause damage of *any kind* to a person, an organisation, a reputation, an animal or the environment, is, for me, an ethical issue.

Interestingly, within my PhD research, Self-Awareness was more highly correlated with Ethics than it was with Self-Regulation, which came as rather a surprise. However, on reflection, we know that students debating an ethical dilemma will make more ethical and pro-social choices once they have had a chance to debate the issue together and hear each other's perspectives. So perhaps my research suggests that by increasing people's levels of self-awareness we can, co-relationally, increase the quality of their ethical decision-making.

The 3 Pillars comprise many different cognitive, emotional and behavioural elements which, taken together, will make each leader authentic in their own way. As I mentioned earlier, Authentic Leadership is correlated with a number of positive organisational outcomes. Of these, trust is the most significant. The association between trust and Authentic Leadership is important for HR practitioners as trust is the virtue that followers identify as the attribute that they most seek in a leader[1]. Moreover, high levels of trust also correlate with improved employee engagement and well-being, increased levels of creativity and problem-solving, reduced employee turnover and greater productivity[2].

The 10 Principles of Authentic Leadership

1. First and foremost, people will be authentic in their own ways regarding their personal leadership style and unique underpinning philosophy of leadership.

2. Authentic Leadership involves leading with *courage*, i.e. emotional and physical bravery and also compassion.

3. Leader *self-awareness* isn't enough; the term also encompasses *other*-awareness and the truly Authentic Leader has both.

4. Trust is an *output* of Authentic Leadership, not an *input*

5. Being yourself isn't enough: Authentic Leaders are their *Best Selves.*

6. You are always a role model, (whether you like it or not). Whatever you do, you give others permission to do.

7. Authentic Leadership is the *sum total* of who you are, what you know, what you believe and what you value.

8. Authentic Leadership is an embodied attitude of mind; it's as much of a way of *being* (in the world), as it is a way of *doing* (leadership).

9. You need to learn to lead yourself, so others choose to follow you; Authentic Leadership is about relationships not power.

10. As Authentic Leadership is *relational*; it concerns the relationship that you have with *yourself* as much as it is about the relationships that you have with *others*.

The 3 Reasons Why Leaders Fail

• They lack Self-Awareness

• They lack Self-Regulation

• They lack Ethics

Remember that a lack of self-awareness will also, by association, include a lack of others-awareness. A lack of judgement regarding Self-Regulation and Self-Control, be that of the CEO of a UK High Street bank who takes cocaine, an American president who ejaculates over an intern's dress, or a married Prime Minister who has an affair with one of his Cabinet Ministers, also shows a lack of awareness regarding the impact that their indiscretions will have. Lying about their behaviour simply highlights a lack of Ethics and the fact that they cannot be trusted to tell the truth.

When I work with groups or present at conferences, I often ask people to describe the *worst* leaders and managers they've ever come across. I have now asked this of many hundreds of people and I have yet to hear an example where the leader's poor thinking or behaviours sat outside of the 3 Pillars of Authentic Leadership. When you think about it, this simplifies the previous chapter on leadership derailers completely.

The next chapter explores Authentic Leadership in Action. It includes 10 case studies of real people, who will bring Authentic Leadership and the Leadership Temperament Types to life for you. They are all Authentic Leaders in their own ways, and it is always an honour and a privilege to work with them and be in their company.

If you would like to learn more about Authentic Leadership there are links to more information and resources, including the UK's only 360 Authentic Leadership profile and report, developed with the UK's Royal Air Force, on the *www.unitedbychocolate.com* website. My doctoral research thesis can be freely downloaded from the British Library's thesis portal *www.ethos.bl.uk.*

Chapter 9: Authentic Leadership in Action

As they are motivated by different things, the four Leadership Temperament Types will lead differently, each being authentic in their own ways. This chapter illustrates how the four Leadership Temperament Types may lead in practice by sharing with you some real stories and the actual scores of genuine leaders in the form of 10 short case studies.

Fisher suggests that people's primary and secondary temperament types are the most important thing in romantic partner selection. My thinking around leaders and leadership is slightly different. While I agree completely that our primary and secondary hormonal drivers are paramount, I have come to believe that all of the temperament types are important. They are important both in terms of the order in which they come, and also in terms of someone's preference levels. For example, if someone's leadership profile is high for being a Director and low for the other three styles, they are going to lead and manage in a very different way to someone who has an equally high preference for the task and success, (Director profile), but who also scores moderately for being people-oriented, (the Negotiator), sustainability, (the Builder), and being involved in exciting projects, (the Explorer).

In the following pages you will find 10 examples of real leaders who have been generous enough to share their stories, and their scores, with us. As I was writing their paragraphs, I became fascinated about the assumptions that you might make about them, even from simply reading their gender and their titles, knowing what you now do about Leadership Temperament Types. One of them is a lawyer, a Partner in a law firm, so is likely to be tough minded. How do your assumptions change when I tell you that this individual is a woman? When I use the word 'volunteer' to describe someone, what ideas do you form about them in your mind in terms of which Leadership Temperament Type/s you think they are likely to be?

Our 10 case studies are:

- Louise Mumford, Chartered Surveyor and Volunteer Trustee

- Julia Cole, Partner in a Law Firm

- Mark, Ex-Military, Entrepreneur and Volunteer Coastguard

- Dr. Julia Hallam-Seagrave, Senior Manager, the National Health Service

- Russell Atkin, Businessman and Volunteer Manager

- Susan Montorano, Hotel HR Executive and Freelance Hotel Consultant

- Peter Treglown, Marketing Executive, PR Consultant and Volunteer Trustee

- Lisa Poole, Interim HR Director and Owner of HR Protocol

- Kevin, Ex-Military, Lloyds Broker, Specialist Project Manager and N.E.D.

- Nicola Wiltshire, Hotel Manager, Private Banking Services Director and Executive Coach

Louise Mumford, Chartered Surveyor and Volunteer Trustee

In elected roles, Louise was Chair of the Royal Institute of Chartered Surveyors (RICS) East Midlands Regional Board for two years and Chair of the RICS Appeals Panel for nine. At the same time she was Chair of Grantham Civic Society for ten years and a Trustee of Grantham's Museum, which was very nearly closed due to government spending cuts a few years ago, but which happily, due to the committed efforts of many people, now remains open. In her day job as a Chartered Surveyor, within her own firm, she specialises in mediating between parties in third-party wall disputes, where the cases are often very complicated indeed, involving multiple parties and high-powered lawyers. Having taken a step back from the RICS so she can spend more time with her family, she is now a local Parish Councillor, a Trustee of her local Village Hall and Chair of the St. John's County Priory Group who organise the volunteer St. John's Ambulance provision for Lincolnshire. In her spare time, for fun, although she has incorporated it into her business, she renovates properties, some of which are commercial offices, some residential, and two of which, Gardener's Cottage and Groom's Cottage, are delightfully pretty holiday accommodation in Norfolk, near to the Queen's Sandringham Estate.

What clues have I given you here as to what Louise's profile might be?

Chairing Committees and the longevity of her roles as the Chair on them suggests Builder. Her commitment to local community projects also suggests Builder. Taking a multiple perspective approach and helping people to resolve third-party wall disputes suggests some Negotiator thinking and behaviours. My inclusion of the word 'fun' might suggest some Explorer tendencies to mitigate the seriousness of a Builder profile, and though I haven't mentioned it explicitly, we can assume it, as she obviously has to be highly organised and at times very focused. Because the firm she works for is her own, and she is therefore the decision maker, there may also be some Director traits present as well. But which Leadership Temperament Type is her primary motivator and which ones play the supporting roles? Before I give you the answers, let's hear from Louise herself, as her words will also give us some insights into her thinking.

Usually the committees I chair have high powered people with quite strong personalities I find it fascinating to watch and listen to them as they all think so differently. It's my role to balance and moderate them to get the best out of them all and draw everyone together, smoothing over any tensions. The Appeals Committee was about being scrupulously fair and ensuring that we got everybody's viewpoint and opinion. Nothing annoys me more than people who sit on a committee and don't say anything! Everyone who's there needs to have a voice, so I ensure that everyone says something and we reach a consensus.

The best committees I've sat on have diverse groups of people. When we're faced with a problem they all see it in completely different ways which is very helpful for the rest of the group. I encourage them to be themselves without being judged. Also, it's very important that the meetings have a purpose and that people enjoy being there and being together, even if the purpose is a serious one. I always ensure that the venue is a pleasant one, that there's enough to eat, that we have regular breaks so that people are comfortable and that there's an element of social interaction so that people can enjoy being there as well as doing some good.

I love doing up cottages and houses. Bricks and mortar excite me! You can't get more solid than bricks and mortar. They are tangible in ways which stocks and shares aren't. I like thinking of people being safe and warm and having a good time in the places that I've done up, and I'm constantly thinking of things that I can do to make the best use of the space. Gardener's Cottage now has a little fairy house built into the corner by the house and Groom's Cottage has a new Norman arched door built into the wall so guests can access the private garden directly from the front without having to go through the house.

It seems then, that all of the four Leadership Temperament Types are present in Louise's language and thinking: the fun elements enjoyed by the Explorer; the nurturing of the Negotiator; the task focus of the Director and the balance beloved by the Builder. Out of a possible 100% on each scale, Louise scored 92% on the Negotiator questions, 88% for the Builder, 52% for the Director and 40% for the Explorer. Because the scores are so close, you may have thought that perhaps she was a Builder/Negotiator. However, if you met her in person, she is so warm and kind and considerate, you would immediately recognise her as a classic Negotiator, making her profile that of a Negotiator/Builder.

Julia Cole, Partner in a Law Firm

A farmer's daughter, Julia surprised some of her friends when she opted to study law at University; however, she saw it as a long-term career option that she would be able to build around having career breaks for children. Of course, at 18, she wasn't planning to have children just yet, but she knew that it was what she wanted to do when the time was right and she met the partner she would settle down with. The law is a solid, safe, ethical and dependable job that she could do anywhere, and whilst she wasn't planning to move away from her family in Lincolnshire, it would provide her with some flexibility if ever she needed it to. Naturally quiet and cautious, she didn't want to play fast and loose with all the risks of having a *portfolio career**, being freelance or with the possibility of not having a career at all, so she deliberately chose reliable and steady law, and stuck with it.

Although she's qualified to practise in all areas of UK law, Julia specialises in property and probate. Unlike in HR or some elements of commercial law, things are steady and the law doesn't change very often. And she wouldn't like the adversarial nature of divorce law, she says. Julia likes developing long-term relationships with her clients and helping them through the process of probate, which is often complicated by tenant farmers and multiple properties being involved, and of course, being in the process of grieving for a loved one means that everyone needs a supporting arm to guide them and, metaphorically, sometimes a hand to hold.

Since having her children she only works part-time, although the firm's other Partners are constantly pushing for her to work full-time, something which she is determined she will never do again. She likes the balance she's been able to achieve, even though she sometimes has to work 'long days', a 12-hour day from 8am to 8pm. But the balance is there, she says, because it's an opportunity for her husband to spend time with the children too. Ultimately, she will always put family first.

In the office the other all-male Partners tease her about being 'an honorary boy', someone who, they feel, looks like a woman but thinks like a man; and if there's ever a difficult conversation to be had with a member of staff about performance, hours, redundancy or being 'let go', then it's invariably Julia who is asked to do it. She doesn't mind; at least that way she can make sure that procedure has been followed and that the person is OK with things being done nicely even if the circumstances are difficult. It's very important to Julia that her reputation, and that of the firm, is a good one, and that she is thought of as reliable, trustworthy, ethical and fair. When you meet her, she comes across as being gentle, intelligent, patient, conscientious, practical, logical, kind, empathetic, positive, generous in her praise and enthusiastic. She's delightful to be around and very reassuring. She loves her role and her clients love her. She's excellent at her job and it seems that her particular combination of Leadership Temperament Types are a recipe for success from everyone's perspective.

Out of a possible 100% for each Type, Julia scores most highly for being a Builder, (96%), then a Negotiator, (88%), and a Director, (80%). She scores moderately for being an Explorer, (52%). Scoring so highly for three out of the four Leadership Temperament Types means that Julia is very flexible. Not only can she get on with everyone, she's also very flexible in her approach at work. The order of her preferences are as important as the level of them, by which I mean she will use solid and reliable and trustworthy Builder strategies first, closely followed by nurturing and caring Negotiator behaviours, all underpinned by logical, pleasantly forthright and practical advice.

----

* It's not unusual nowadays to have had more than one career or to have what's known as a *portfolio career* where multiple job roles form one combined income. From what you've learned about Temperament Types I expect you can guess which type is most likely to have a portfolio career. (I would predict that it would be an Explorer, as they would enjoy the excitement of it and feel that they could cope with the potential risk.) I would also suggest that you could predict the Temperament Type that would be least likely to have a portfolio career as well. (I think it would be the Builder, who would hate the lack of stability, firm foundations and the security of one stable income with holiday and sickness pay.)

Let me introduce you to Mark, who, in contrast to Julia the lawyer, has had three consecutive careers so far.

Mark, Ex-Military, Entrepreneur and Volunteer Coastguard

As a young man, Mark spent a number of years as a professional soldier, seeing active service in a variety of places around the world in the defence of his country. For many servicemen and women, life after living in an exclusively military environment can be quite difficult to adjust to. This wasn't the case for Mark. After years of having to follow orders, he decided to become the boss and set up his own company using his specialist knowledge in search and rescue. He wanted to create an organisation which would not only benefit society, but which was built to last, and through good leadership, exceptional results and a good reputation, would grow organically. His leadership style was to develop long-term, sustainable relationships with multi-agency clients and to involve every member of staff collaboratively in growing the company by utilising everyone's combined knowledge and expertise.

One of Mark's other strategies was to ensure that, despite the long hours and often very serious and quite difficult work, the crews enjoyed themselves as much as possible in the downtime between search and rescue projects. The company did indeed flourish and continues to do so today, even after Mark sold it on so that he could spend more time pursuing his own projects, particularly his passion for overland travel to far-flung places.

When he's not exploring the world and everything in it, Mark is a volunteer Coastal Rescue Officer for Her Majesty's Coastguard, where his specialist knowledge and expertise in search and rescue are enormously valuable in the training and development and support of his colleagues. Let's hear from Mark himself.

My leadership style has changed over the years. In the military I was much more directive. That was the only framework we were given, so that was the only way we knew how to behave. But after three decades of work and experience I've now become a completely different kind of leader.

I felt most myself when I was CEO of the Search and Rescue organisation. The level of professionalism and engagement was second to none. We were a band of brothers. I valued them and they valued me. My style was one of, 'This is what I would suggest, what would everyone else suggest?' and so the team shared the tactical platform as well as the operational one. I used to say to them, "Don't just bring me the problems, think them through and bring me solutions and I will support you. If you want my input, just ask".

To better understand Mark's Leadership Temperament Types I profiled him in two different ways. Firstly, I invited him to answer a *forced choice* questionnaire, made up of a set of 16 lines of four words, one word representing each Temperament Type. He could choose only one word from each line. Secondly, I invited him to complete the same questionnaire again, but this time he could select *any and all* of the words which he felt either described him or were important to him.

The first profile, with the forced choices, identifies someone's values. When everything else is stripped away, what's most important to them becomes clear. Or at least it becomes clear if you make the effort to speak with them about what's important to them and why. One of the interesting things about values is that they can often be hidden, obscured by someone's cognitive and behavioural flexibility, as you will see in a moment with Mark's rather unusual profile.

I'm going to give you Mark's scores backwards so I can explain to you what I mean. When he could select any and all of the words which were meaningful to him, Mark scores 100% for Explorer, suggesting, as we already know, that originality and innovation, excitement, adventure, adrenalin, spontaneity, freedom, enthusiasm, bravery, having fun and exploring options and possibilities at work are all important to him. His secondary Leadership Preference Type is that of the Negotiator, for which he also scores very highly at 96%, meaning that at work he is warm, supportive, caring, compassionate, intuitive, generous, encouraging, kind, collaborative, altruistic and people-focused. Mark's Director and Builder scores are also both very high, at 92% each. This suggests that the order in which he uses the strategies of Director and Builder will depend on the situation and circumstances that he finds himself in. We know that where appropriate, and if necessary, Mark is very capable of taking the lead in the classic sense of taking charge and being in control, being directive, logical, focused, tough-minded, pragmatic, forthright, determined, bold, influential and powerful; in short, a force to be reckoned with. And we also know that he will always be patient, fair, honest, trustworthy, reliable, ethically resolute, solid, stable and honourable.

So if you were to work with Mark, would you be able to identify what his Values profile is? Probably not, because his behaviour will be so flexible across all four of the Leadership Temperament Types that it would be difficult to recognise what his underlying drivers are. Although, of course, if you pay attention and know what you're looking for, you would be able to tell quite easily when he was in a directive and focused, task-oriented, Director mode, the caring, collaborative and considerate Negotiator mode, the solid and reliable, reassuring, trustworthy Builder mode or his energetic, enthusiastic and fun-loving Explorer mode. Not the ultimate chameleon, but rather, the ultimately flexible colleague who can fit into any team, or indeed lead any team, to achieve whatever needs to be done.

Of course, we have the advantage of knowing something else about Mark. From a Leadership Temperament Types perspective, we do know what his values and underlying motivational drivers are. When forced to choose between words which relate to each Type, Mark only scores 6% for Explorer, quite a surprise compared to the 100% he scores the second time he completes the questionnaire. This suggests that in a high-pressure environment or in a crisis situation, this absolutely isn't a mode of thinking or behaving he will go into. He scores 18% for Builder and 26% for Director, meaning that his predominant driver, first and foremost, is always going to be that of the people-focused Negotiator, for which he scores the remaining 50%.

Mark's comparatively high Negotiator score might explain why, when he completed a series of tests at the UK's Fire Service College, which is the centre of training operations for the UK's Fire Rescue Service, his score for what's called *protective instinct* was one of the highest they had ever seen. He describes it as having *'a rescue head'*, and it goes a long way towards explaining why he, as a volunteer, and like every other Coastal Rescue Officer in Her Majesty's Coastguard, is prepared to be on call 24/7 and will drop everything at a moment's notice to try to save the life of anyone who is in danger around the UK coastline.

This is what Mark has to say about the theory of Leadership Temperament Types.

If you understand someone's leadership style you get a bit of a mind map as to the kind of results that are likely to emerge from them at the other end. The questions you ask in Chapter 5 are very powerful. I reckon that you're on to something, I really do. It makes complete sense to me.

Mark's case study is a great example of the value and usefulness of being able to complete the questionnaire in two different ways to yield a uniquely different set of results, and to be able to use those to understand how someone is likely to lead and manage.

Dr Julia Hallam-Seagrave, Senior Manager, the National Health Service

Julia has worked as a dentist within the National Health Service (NHS) since she qualified more than twenty years ago. Taking every opportunity for training and development and willingly accepting greater clinical responsibility, she rose quickly up the ranks to lead a team of highly qualified and committed professionals. The NHS is an exciting, high-pressure, numbers-focused, multi-agency environment well recognised for being both rewarding and yet also an incredibly difficult and complex place to work. It is highly procedural and the information systems are often so convoluted that staff can take years to fully understand them, especially as they are constantly changing! It would be very easy for Julia to go into private practice and work fewer hours for greater pay; however, she absolutely refuses to do so. She would miss her patients too much, she says, and besides, they need her. When she's not riding her horse around a cross-country course or training for a marathon, her holidays are often spent providing free dental treatment to children in Romanian orphanages.

So what do you think we know about Julia so far? Let's hear what she has to say.

Over the years I've become much less people-focused and much more task-focused due to the stress and pressures of the job and my more senior leadership responsibilities. I have to make sure I meet my targets and that other people do as well. I like myself less now compared to five years ago and I do think about how people perceive me now compared to how I was. My people-focus is overridden by pressure from above and the need to do a job. Sometimes there's a clash between my head and my heart and the decisions I would really rather be making. Clinical decisions are easy. I can be much more directive and there's no conflict. It's only where my staff are involved that I sometimes struggle a bit. But we are all constantly adapting aren't we? It would be really interesting to do this again in five years' time or when I have another role.

In her present job, on a 100% scale for each Leadership Temperament Type, Julia scores 88% for being Directive/Transactional. This isn't really a surprise when we consider how much of her working life is task and results oriented and numbers focused. Her evident conflict comes because she also scores 84% for Relational and being a Negotiator, and whilst there is a difference in her scores, the 4% is unlikely to be a significant difference, meaning that sometimes her motivational drivers may clash. She also scores 80% for being an Explorer, something which she feels is really helpful as she says that she is often running on adrenalin at work and can see patients for up to 13 hours a day, from 7am until 8pm. Her Builder score is 64% and reflects her high ethics, reliability, loyalty to her patients and the NHS, and her pro-social nature.

Julia has some more to say about the process of completing her profile and some advice for you as the reader.

While the profile is predominantly work-related, there's also quite a lot of personal stuff in it too which is really interesting. Doing the questionnaire has helped me by giving me more awareness of what's going on for me when I'm leading a team, and it's also helped me to understand and manage my boss who's very different to me. My advice to readers is to be honest when completing the questionnaire because it works! It's highlighted to me something that I really need to address, ... that I do have this inner conflict between what I would like to do and what I have to do. I suppose the next step is to use it to develop my own leadership so that I can become more comfortable and confident with my leadership decisions rather than being confused as to where my inner conflict comes from. Instead of wondering, 'Why am I thinking/feeling like this?', now I know, and that's really helpful.

Russell Atkin, Businessman and Volunteer Manager

Russell is another example of an Authentic Leader whose internal values are very clear to him and those who know him very well, but may not be apparent to those people who encounter him generally at work. Russell has an interesting profile, as his underlying values are potentially in conflict: he's an Explorer/Builder. You will remember from the grid in Chapter 3 that the characteristics in these two Leadership Temperament Type styles can appear, potentially, to be in opposition.

Russell's profile is a good example of the fact that any and all combinations of Leadership Temperament Types are possible, and that they don't have to clash!

Let's explore Russell's full profile and see what emerges. His forced choice questionnaire gives a score of 10% for the Transactional Director, 25% for the Relational Negotiator, 30% for the Transformational Builder and 35% for the Charismatic Explorer. As Russell's profile is unusual, I will share with you some of the words he selected from the forced choice questionnaire so you can see how his profile is complementary rather than contradictory: Family; Reputation; Reliable; Loyal; Dutiful; Having Fun; Excitement; Bravery; Freedom; Adventure and Adrenalin.

For Russell, family always come first; no exceptions. Family is his highest priority, and as an entrepreneur who relies on his reputation, that is also very important to him; both of these are Builder characteristics. However, once family and reputation are secure, other things become important, like adventure, freedom and having fun. When Russell organises a party everyone comes. So what happens to Russell's scores when he can choose any and all of the words that apply to him?

Then Russell's profile changes from an Explorer/Builder to become an Explorer/Director. He scores 90% for the Charismatic Explorer, 85% for the Transactional Director, 70% for the Relational Negotiator and 60% for the Transformational Builder. I've known and worked with Russell for more than 15 years and I've had the opportunity to see his working style at first hand. He's excellent at building long-term relationships. People are important to him and he takes a great interest in them. For their part, people want to please him and they value his good opinion. He's generous, caring and considerate and will always help someone if he can. He's the best manager and leader of volunteers I have ever met.

Interestingly, Russell isn't charismatic in the recognised way that perhaps we might think of charisma, people like Richard Branson or, arguably, Former President of the USA, Bill Clinton. He is what I would describe as quietly charismatic. He's very decisive and people naturally defer to him. That's quite natural as he is the boss; however, even when he's not in his formal leadership role, people still look to him for advice, reassurance and support and follow his lead. He has a natural ability to resolve any issue. He never shies away from difficult conversations and is both physically brave as well as emotionally brave, without ever becoming aggressive. There is a feeling of security around him; the people within his circle, whether they are friends, employees, volunteers or clients, feel absolutely and completely safe within his protectorate. When he's in the building, everyone relaxes. He is the leader; he's in charge and he's absolutely in control, so no one else needs to be alert to any danger. 'Team Russ' is a great place to be.

Susan Martorano, HR Executive and Hotel Consultant

There's a newspaper cutting that Susan keeps in a drawer at home. It says, 'Axe woman comes to ****', and it refers to a time when she had to close a tourist attraction in Scotland, terminating the contracts of all 80 employees in order to make way for a new hotel complex. Commercially, she would rather simply have moved the whole enterprise along the road or even into the hotel complex itself; however, that decision wasn't hers to make and so the job of Axe Woman was indeed hers.

How do you think Susan would have handled the situation if she had been a Director / Transactional Leader? How might she have behaved differently if she were a Builder / Transformational Leader or if she had a Relational Leadership / Negotiating style preference? What would the Charismatic Explorer have done? Even being able to consider these questions from the perspective of the four different Leadership Temperament Types will indicate just how much you've learned since you first turned the front cover of this book.

Let me give you Susan's scores and share with you the process and eventual outcome of the closure. Susan has an *adapted self* at work, so it's an interesting read. In the forced choice questionnaire Susan scores 18% for each of the following three styles: Explorer; Director and Builder. The remaining 46% is her Negotiator score. So in terms of her *values*, what's going on inside for her, Susan is very caring and concerned about people. However, unless she knew you well enough and trusted you enough to reveal her true values to you, what you would see, and what her colleagues see, is her *professional face* – the persona she needs to be at work in order to do her job effectively. Most of us have a difference between the way that we are at home and with our friends and the way we feel that we need to be at work. It's a form of legitimate self-protection: a coping strategy if you like, and for many of us, it feels as comfortable to slip on in the morning as the coat we put on to go out of the door.

In the second questionnaire, when each of the four Leadership Temperament Types could potentially achieve 100%, Susan scores 62% for Explorer; 68% for Builder; 75% for Negotiator and a high 88% for Director. How do you think that she might come across if you were to meet her in person? Let's hear from Susan herself.

In questionnaires for work, I always come out as a natural leader and people don't necessarily see the caring and nurturing side of me. It's something that I've deliberately encouraged at work over the years. I don't want to come across as more caring because at work, especially in HR, you can become vulnerable and people can take advantage of you and exploit your kind nature. Some people, when they realise that you're very people-focused, can try and manipulate you, and I've found that they respect you more if you come across as being a bit more results-oriented and directive. I always make my decisions based on the effect and impact that things are going to have on people, but I don't let people know that. I'm aware that it's a self-protection mechanism, but I've seen it happen to other people where they have been taken advantage of so I'm deliberately harder on the outside. I don't experience any conflict at all! It feels completely natural to me. I'm still 'me' on the inside.

Regarding the closure of the tourist attraction at ****, even though it wasn't my decision, I felt that I had a professional responsibility to make it right for everybody. I gave myself way more work than I needed to do, but it was really important to me that everyone was OK. I spent a lot of time with people, even coaching people individually. I involved the local council and other local businesses and I made sure that everyone who wanted another job got one. Some people chose to retire, a couple went back to college to learn new skills and one set up their own business that they'd been wanting to do for years. I helped all of them without making a fuss about it.

I've moved on from HR now. With my background and experience in the hotel industry I'm a freelance Hotel Consultant. I'm like a mystery guest. I check in and stay as a guest and use all the amenities, chatting to both the staff and the other guests. I find out about staff attitudes and morale as happy and helpful staff means happy guests, good feedback and repeat visits. I feed back to the hotel senior management regarding the quality of the guest experience. Then I work with them on all of the systems and procedures and the training that they need to put in place so that their guests have a better experience and they get improved feedback and ratings on Trip Advisor and other such sites. It works to all of my strengths and it's a win/win all round.

Peter Treglown, Marketing and PR Consultant and Trustee

Peter has worked as a volunteer for the same organisation for nearly 50 years, starting at the bottom and working with many other volunteers to turn a small interest group and start-up venture, driven by passion and commitment, into a £3 million turnover business. Those volunteers then formed a charity to take over from the commercial business. The charity is the South Devon Railway Trust and as a major tourist venue, it now attracts more than a hundred thousand visitors annually.

As is so often the case with the kind of people who volunteer their time and energy so willingly and so generously, the South Devon

Railway isn't the only charity which Peter has actively supported over the years. He's been a Parish Councillor, and was Chairman of his local Village Hall Committee for six years, helping to raise funds of £350,000 to build the village hall as a centre for the community. In his spare time, not that he has much of that, he also sits on his local Neighbourhood Plan committee and used to sit on the committee of his local rugby club helping them to improve their communications and media profile. He now helps organise their annual rugby sevens tournament. This is an impressive volunteering CV, especially when we also consider that Peter works up to a 60 hour week running his own successful marketing and PR company and employs ten people.

I've had the good fortune to work with Peter for many years. In fact, it was his design studio which created the diagrams in this book. He's brilliant to work with; he balances my needs as a client with all of his other clients, so deadlines are always met and we can all relax. He's very much the expert in the room, which is always reassuring. I've never known him not be able to come up with a creative solution to a problem! Over the years he has built an excellent team around him and as a client I can feel confident in all of them.

From what I've said, you've probably been able to guess some of Peter's Leadership Temperament Type preferences from his life and career, so let's hear from Peter himself and then I will share his scores with you.

You may have heard of the Beeching cuts, … Dr Beeching closed a lot of railway lines in the 1960's and my dad and I used to go round and visit the closed ones when we were on holiday. When I was 13 we walked round a corner in Devon and saw a man painting a level crossing gate, and that was it! I wanted to be a part of what the whole organisation was doing, so I joined as a volunteer and spent many of my holidays learning new skills and being around the steam trains. I joined in 1967 and the line re-opened in 1969.

I'm still an active volunteer, albeit now as a Director and Trustee, in fact I do something for them every day one way or another but I don't get to go down very often to get my hands dirty as I now live 350 miles away! Many of our current volunteers will know my name but not who I am. I ought to resign as a Trustee really, because I live so far away, but I can still add value and play my part on the Board to do things better, so all the time I can do that I'll stay. My main role is in strategic marketing plus day-to-day marketing and communications: something I'm trying to get some more people involved in but everyone wants to do the exciting stuff, they're not really interested in checking Facebook or Trip Advisor every day to see what people have written about the café, but it's still a job that needs to be done!

At work, the nature of what I do is all about building a client's brand and reputation so of course relationships and relationship building is really important to me. We will only be successful if our clients are successful and the whole team works very hard at that. It's important for me to respect my clients and what they achieve; after all, we need to build a mutually beneficial relationship and that involves collaboration on both sides. We very rarely lose a client. There are the very occasional ones one feels a little uncomfortable working with. I suppose you could describe them as the control freaks, the ones that like to have their hand in everything. I have had experience of such people upsetting members of staff quite unreasonably and that's just unforgivable in my book. It's bullying behaviour, which I abhor. People say that business isn't personal but of course it is, at least to some extent. We all have feelings and emotions and it's important to wake up and want to come to work. I enjoy my job and I want my team to feel the same way.

So what clues are there for you here from Peter himself? If you guessed that Peter's preferences regarding his values are Builder/Negotiator, then well done! Let's review his actual scores, because they are interesting and shed more light on his leadership style. Using the same two questionnaires that we used for Mark, when Peter completed the forced choice questionnaire of having to choose between the four Leadership Temperament Types, he scored 18% for both Explorer and Director, and 32% for both Negotiator and Builder. It's impossible to know which comes first as the scores are identical, however his volunteering, the way he talks and the language he uses certainly seem to suggest Builder as a first preference.

Let's see what happens when Peter can select all of the words in the questionnaire which he feels describe him. Now we will get a profile of Peter's flexibility and the way that other people will perceive him at work. So what happens? Interestingly there are no tied scores this time. Peter's lowest preference is Charismatic Explorer, for which he has a preference score of 50% out of a possible 100%. Looking more carefully at the words he has selected I can tell that whilst he enjoys creativity and likes to have fun at work, he won't take any undue risks and he's not motivated by last minute deadlines and adrenaline. His next lowest preference score is for the Relational Negotiator at 63%. This is still quite a high score and suggests, as we've already heard from Peter himself, that relationships are important to him and he works hard at developing and maintaining them.

Transactional Director Leadership strategies score 69%, again quite a high score. As Peter himself said, he likes to be able to influence decisions, and listening to Peter, it seems that he does need to be directive, results focused, confident and decisive in his day-to-day role. He just does it warmly and considerately rather than being demanding or overly-directive. As you might have predicted, at 82% Peter scores most highly for being a Builder and using Transformational strategies to lead as a first preference. This is completely consistent with his values and is, I would suggest, Authentic Leadership in action.

www.fouragency.co.uk   *www.southdevonrailway.co.uk*

Lisa Poole, Interim HR Director and owner of HR Protocol

Lisa worked in the arena of Human Resources for many years before setting up her own business providing HR consultancy and workplace mediation services to small and medium-sized businesses which can't afford, or don't need, a full-time HR Director.

My approach has changed with age and circumstances. Historically, when I was employed in HR there was always someone above me and there wasn't really any difference between how I was at work and how I was at home. There's a big difference now between how I am at home and how I am at work, and I feel much more 'me' at work and I'm much happier, probably because I take all of the decisions. I'm much more of a presence at work and I seem to be a role model for other people as to how they should be behaving professionally. I would like to think so anyway.

I've had to pull myself up to my full height as my clients have expected more of me. My role now is much more directive, as I'm expected to make decisions and take more responsibility. I will always go for a people-focused approach first as a preference as I've found over the years that it works better, but if that approach doesn't work I will go down the directive route and tell it like it is. I don't have any difficulty with that, in fact I find it very easy, but I would prefer not to have to get tough with people, I don't feel that I should need to. It is an approach I have to take with some Boards though as that seems to be the only language they understand and they won't respect me or my views if I'm not forthright with them.

It seems from what Lisa has said that there are some Negotiator and Director behaviours going on in her profile. We can't tell which without looking more closely at her scores, although Lisa's comment about feeling most herself when she can make all of the decisions might give us a clue! Let's have a look at Lisa's scores using the forced choice questionnaire to identify her values first, and then let's look at her flexibility and approach in practice.

In the forced choice questionnaire identifying her inner values, Lisa scores 6% for Explorer and 19% for Builder. She scores 25% for Negotiator and the remaining 50% for Director. For the second questionnaire, out of a possible 100% for each Leadership Temperament Type, Lisa scores 88% for Director as her first preference, 81% for Negotiator, 68% for Builder and 37% for Explorer. The order of her preferences is consistent across both questionnaires. Are these scores a surprise to you? Is the order of her scores a surprise to you? They're not for me, having met Lisa. She is intelligent, forthright, considered, accurate, independently minded, calm, balanced, non-emotional, factual, quietly influential and decisive, focused and logical. She's pleasant without any need to please and she's the ultimate professional. She knows that she's in the room sitting at the table and advising the Board because of the quality of her thinking. Using Baron-Cohen's terminology, Lisa has a predominantly 'male' brain in a female body. From my perspective, and from the perspective of everyone who meets her, Lisa is another example of Authentic Leadership in Action.

www.hrprotocol.co.uk

Kevin, Ex-Military, Lloyds Broker, Specialist Project Manager and Non-Executive Director (NED)

After military training at Sandhurst, Kevin spent 20 years in the army and army reserves leading teams of upwards of 100 people. He knew them all individually – not just their names but also their strengths and weaknesses. He made it his business to, not only because he genuinely cared about each and every one of them, but because doing so gave him a tactical advantage when planning operations. Calmly intelligent, complexity is something that Kevin really enjoys. Throughout his career, and most recently in his freelance specialist project management role, he has had the ability to be able to manage and juggle the outcomes of the client with the demands of the project and the needs of the project team. This is never an easy task, especially when projects often span different geographical locations and multiple time zones and when the project team is also a diverse, multi-cultural one.

Kevin specialises in Customer Relationship Management projects for large organisations where the desired outcomes and results are complex but clear, albeit multi-faceted; where the approach is consultative and people oriented, where there is a need for a unique intellectual input to ensure continued results over the longer term, and where the systems and processes coalesce seamlessly with the people who have to use them.

What clues do we have about Kevin's preferences from what I've described about Kevin so far? The words 'longer term', 'relationships' and 'intellectual' are the important ones here. And if you were to meet Kevin in person you would find him to be calm, considered, logical, rational, patient, considerate, independently minded, collaborative, quietly determined, practical, collaborative, interested in your views and opinions and generous with his time and in his praise.

I profiled Kevin using the forced choice questionnaire I've described earlier where one word out of four is selected from each of 16 lines, and then I profiled him for a second time using the same questionnaire but where any and all of the words which he felt applied to him could be selected. His scores were interesting. For Kevin, like Russell and Mark, what occurs on the inside privately, regarding his motivational drivers and values, are not necessarily what his colleagues might think that they are, based on the flexibility and breadth of his behaviours when they are working with him.

Regarding his internal values, Kevin scores 12% for Explorer and 19% for Negotiator. He scores 31% for Director and 37% for Builder. His predominant Builder preference is a reflection of his high ethics and the fact that he will always put his family first. At work, and out of a possible 100% score for each Leadership Temperament Type, Kevin scores 56% for being a Charismatic Explorer, as well as 56% for being the stoic, ethical and reliable Transformational Builder. He scores 75% for the Relational Negotiator and the highest 100% for the Transactional Director. So, at work, his colleagues will experience him being very results oriented, but in a highly supportive way.

I particularly wanted to include Kevin's profile in this chapter so I could show how even a 100% score for a directive Transactional leadership style can be tempered when it's mediated by some of the other Leadership Temperament Types. Statistically, a Director/Negotiator profile is quite rare, although I have a feeling that Kevin's military training at Sandhurst and his early career history as a peacekeeper may also have shaped the kind of leader that he is today. Let's hear from Kevin himself. I asked him a bit more about his early career and his peacekeeping role.

Relationships are key. It's important to keep up a constant dialogue with people and to allow face-saving on both sides. You can't start from a position of weakness. Whilst never being aggressive yourself in any way, the other side has to know that you are unwavering. You have to be firm and remain firm and be very clear about the outcomes that need to be achieved. You have to be calm, patient and focused as it can be a slow process and trust needs to be built on both sides. That takes time and one wrong word can undo weeks and months of work so understanding the complexities of the situation and the complex personalities of the people involved is also critical.

Obviously my role now is hugely different to what it was then, but an ability to remain calmly focused on the results while taking your people with you, is, I think, an invaluable skill in any leadership position.

Nicola Wiltshire, Hotel Manager, Private Banking Services Director and Executive Coach

Making the transition from Hotel Manager to Private Banker in one of the UK's most prestigious private banking firms isn't a career switch that many people have made, but Nicola made it with ease and very quickly rose up the banking hierarchy to become one of the bank's youngest senior executives. This was all the more remarkable as Nicola is quiet and unassuming, a classic introvert when the majority or senior executives in the organisation could be described as extroverts. They are loud, confident, outgoing, even brash sometimes.

When Nicola attended the senior executive development programme a few years ago she scored in the top quartile for her performance against a population sample of more than 200 senior executives who had previously attended the course. Her strengths include: organisational and cultural insight, building capability, strategic influence, understanding and energising others, leveraging relationships, focusing on results, building business intelligence and driving action.

Her role in the bank covered the service and delivery channels, including all of the customer service elements, media, operations and PR. She was two levels down from the main Board, had responsibility for 230 staff and a budget in excess of £8 million – impressive when we consider that she achieved all of this while still in her mid-30s. So what was it about Nicola's leadership style which made her so successful? Let's have a look at her scores to see if they can offer us any insight into her success.

Out of a possible 100%, Nicola scores a very high 94% for Relational Leadership. A classic Negotiator, people always come first; whether it's the client or her staff team, everything that Nicola does is people focused. That's not to say that Nicola isn't also results-focused: she is. In fact, she wouldn't have survived in the bank if she hadn't been. She scores 75% for being directive, action-oriented, decisive and influential. However, Director is her third preference; Nicola's second preference is that of the Transformational Builder for which she scores 82%, suggesting that everything that Nicola does is designed for sustainability, replicability and the longer term. Let's hear what Nicola says as she offers some advice for younger managers and leaders on their way up the career ladder.

Fairness is important. Even when you have to make difficult business decisions and you can't please everyone, it's still important to treat people as people and to be considerate. You have to manage the whole person; you can't just concentrate on the bits that you want from them, you have to support all of them.

Understanding people is critical too. If you don't understand someone how can you get the best out of them? It's like your computer or your mobile phone; if you don't understand how they work you're never going to get the best out of them are you? They've got so much more operating capacity and functionality than you're probably aware of so you only use half of their capability when in reality they have the potential to do so much more if only you knew how to work them properly.

After many years of commuting and working weekends, Nicola has now left the banking sector and opted for a change of pace and a change of lifestyle.

I often used to feel like I was a fish swimming upstream at the bank. A lot of the managers around me and above me had a very different profile to mine and there was a lot of competitive jostling for position and politics which I could deal with but found wearing after a while. I feel much happier in my executive coaching role. When you can do things that you believe in and you can do them to your own standards it's much easier all round as well as being more rewarding personally. Otherwise it's like wearing someone else's shoes; even if they're the same size, they're never really going to quite fit are they?

Nicola is a member of the Association for Coaching and is licensed to use Thinking Styles™, Cognitive Team Roles™ and the Authentic Leadership 360™. She can be contacted via the Cognitive Fitness website at *www.cognitivefitness.co.uk.*

Chapter 10: The Future of the Boardroom

The future of Boardrooms in the UK is undoubtedly going to change, and for the better.

The 2015 Davies Report, *Improving the Gender Balance on British Boards*, confirms that UK FTSE 100 Boards have made significant strides forwards in terms of their percentage of female representation, and therefore, we would hope, also in terms of their operational and strategic perspectives and their overall flexibility.

I am certain that, with continued government support, the UK FTSE 350 companies will reach their target of 33% female representation by 2020, which will lead the way for all Boards and senior teams in small, medium and large commercial organisations to have at least one in four of its members as female.

However, as I said in Chapter 2, this isn't really the point.

While I agree wholeheartedly that diversity pays enormous dividends in terms of increased creativity, innovation, problem-solving and overall productivity, what we really need in commerce, education, charities and the public sector, is diversity of thinking, and greater flexibility, not necessarily diversity of gender! Gender is just one part of the complex jigsaw which makes organisations what they are. Increasing the gender balance on Boards may go some way towards achieving a more thoughtful, pro-social, multi-perspective and balanced approach, or it may not; depending on who is appointed and what their leadership style is.

Equally, not all organisations want to be more pro-social; they may pay lip-service to corporate social responsibility because it's one of the boxes which it's politically expedient to tick, whilst all the time they continue to chase market share, turnover, cost reductions and profitability. The banking and finance sector is a case in point. It's driven by the people at the top, and to get to the top ruthlessness and competitiveness are rewarded. If that wasn't true, we wouldn't have the banking and financial scandals that we do - scenarios which people like our case studies Kevin and Nicola could have predicted, and undoubtedly did predict, except that no-one was listening.

We need more Authentic Leadership and we need more Authentic Leaders. Paradoxically, they are all around us if only we knew how to find and identify them. I would argue that now, we do know how to recognise them: a combination of the 3 Pillars model and the new theory of Leadership Temperament Types can help us to do just that. It's not the complete answer. Intelligence, experience and other things are, and will always be, critical to the mix. However, we have, with this new theory of leadership and leadership style, taken a considerable step forwards.

This chapter now goes on to give you some guidance and direction regarding the following three areas:

- Team and Board development

- Organisational leadership development

- Individual leadership development

Team and Board Development

What kind of a Board do you have? Is it *balanced*, by which I mean are all four Leadership Temperament Types represented by people who genuinely respect each other, or is it (as is often the case) over-heavy on the Transactional Director Leadership scale?

As a *process*, the following 5-Point Plan can be used for all groups and teams, not just the most senior team. The way that I've described it may appear deceptively simple, so do involve someone with some experience and expertise in individual and team development to support you. This 5-Point Plan assumes that everyone who is on the Board or in the team, *should* be there in terms of functionality, technical expertise and intelligence. All of the elements of the process are important, and you need to implement each of them effectively if you want to achieve meaningful, useful, and sustainable results.

A 5-Point Plan for Team Development and Board Success:
1.   Profile the Team.

Profile the people you have on the Board so you understand how it's made up in terms of Temperament Types and leadership styles. Remember, knowing someone's underlying values is as useful as understanding their cognitive and behavioural flexibility. I would strongly recommend that you use the word choice questionnaire on the book's website, *www.unitedbychocolate.com*, as this will also include an individual development report. How many Charismatic, Relational, Transactional and Transformational Leaders do you actually have? What are people's secondary and third choices and how flexible are they? Are there some people who tend to dominate discussions or does everyone share the floor equally?

2.   Understand the *Balance*

Understand what the make-up of your Board actually means for the organisation.   Regardless of gender, if you have a *balanced* Board, with all four Temperament Types and therefore all four leadership styles represented on the Board, the combination that you have might be just fine. Pay particular attention to any potential weaknesses or derailers that the Board might have. Remember, one particularly difficult person could derail the whole Board, making it much less effective over both the short and longer terms.

3. Address the Gaps

Once you understand the make-up of your Board or team, you need to address the gaps. Consider carefully which leadership styles might be missing and develop a recruitment and selection process which will enable you to fill the gaps with the right people, regardless of their gender! Remember, it's Leadership Temperament Types you are recruiting for; you are not looking to fill a gender shortfall! Of course, if you want to use this exercise to address a gender imbalance at the same time, it's an excellent opportunity to do so; however, I'm going to assume that you are going to select the right *person* for the job, regardless of gender, age, race, creed and so on.

A high proportion of external appointments fail. This won't happen if you recruit properly by finding the right people and then supporting them so that they are fully integrated into the culture, ethos and practical day-to-day workings of the organisation.

4. Group Dynamics

Not only must you now induct the person or people effectively into the team, (and possibly into the organisation too if they are an external appointment), you must also introduce them into Board membership in the right way. The internal dynamics of the group will be affected by any new people and so you need to allow for the Forming and Storming of the group before you will reach the Performing stage. (If this doesn't make any sense to you, have a look at the book's website *www.unitedbychocolate.com* for more information and assistance on how to understand and manage the process of group dynamics).

The major danger within any group populated by strong personalities is that they will clash. Disagreement and conflict is fine within a group, provided that a process exists for using the energy it provides to advantage and then moving beyond it without feathers being ruffled and relationships damaged.

5.   Ongoing Programme of Development

Many, but by no means all, senior teams and Boards are dysfunctional in some way.   Often this is because it was individual functional expertise and not an open, flexible or collaborative mindset that got people a seat on the Board in the first place. You need to ensure that the Board members respect and trust each other and that they collaborate together for the sake of the organisation rather than competing with each other.

Always have an ongoing programme of Board development; both for individual Board members and also for the Board as a whole. Involve the Human Resources function and the Training Department by all means, but it's also critical to also ask the Board to assist in the design of the programme so that they buy into it and get the real development that they want, rather than feeling that the programme is something which is being 'done' to them because they are lacking in some way.

If you don't already have it in place, you might also consider a coaching and a mentoring scheme. Senior teams and especially Boards are some of your most expensive assets; it's worth looking after them. Everyone needs a coach, regardless of their seniority. The important thing is to select the right coach for each person or not only will an opportunity be wasted but a lot of time, effort and other resources will be wasted as well.

This 5-Point Plan is an excellent process for facilitating senior team or Board development, but what do you do if you want to develop greater leadership capability more widely across the organisation?

Developing Authentic Leadership at an Organisational Level

Use the following Steps:

1. Underpinning Philosophy

Whilst often overlooked, the first, and most obvious, point is that this needs to be a deliberate strategic decision. Getting the underpinning philosophy right is critical to the success of any development programme. The most effective development programmes reflect the beliefs and values of the organisation. BP is a good example of this; officially launched on the 1st January 2012, its revised Code of Conduct and its five values of Safety, Respect, Excellence, Courage and One team now embody everything that the organisation and its people do.

2. Programme and Design: The 3 Pillars Model

Design the leadership development programme around the 3 Pillars of Authentic Leadership, making the connections and links between all of the programme elements clear. Too often participants are expected to somehow work it all out for themselves as they make sense of a course in their own ways. This means that some people get more out of the experience than others, there is a lack of consistency regarding learning outcomes and application and, worst case scenario, some people may miss the point completely!

In the very best programmes, learning is reinforced and supported in a variety of ways. Leader self-awareness, for example, will be supported by 360° feedback, done at the beginning and end of a programme so changes in colleague and follower perceptions of leadership performance can be tracked. 1:1 coaching and a supportive buddy system which encourages reflection is always beneficial for participant learning, and real-time, 'live' projects can be focused around pro-social, community issues, specific organisational problems or ethical considerations, all of which will increase the intrinsic value of the programme and embed wider learning.

3. Programme Length

The programme needs to be long enough! The majority of leadership development programmes last for five days or less. This simply isn't long enough to embed learning or allow for any kind of real reflection or cognitive and behavioural change. A programme of regular and planned inputs, over six months or ideally a year, with a group of people you can trust, is a much more powerful way to develop positive leadership and an effective leadership pipeline than a few *ad hoc* away-days labelled 'leadership development'.

4. Select the right Participants and the right Facilitators

It's very important that the organisation selects both the right people to attend the programme and also the right people to run it. The trainers/facilitators/coaches will be role models for the courses they are involved with and, if they are not knowledgeable, experienced, likeable, supportive and authentic, the course participants will soon realise and the efficacy of the programme will be diminished.

Likewise, selecting participants is another strategic decision; is inclusion company-wide or limited by certain criteria such as grade or potential? Will differing levels of leadership/management be included? Is the purpose general leadership development or to grow the pipeline of future potential senior leaders? Do participants need to apply and make a case for attending, or will they simply be selected and told to attend?

All of the answers to these questions should be transparent and be clearly linked to the Underpinning Philosophy of the programme and organisational values. If they are not, then the programme will be muddled and, whilst it may be an *authentic* programme, it won't be an *Authentic Leadership* programme.

5. Ongoing Review

Building in an open and transparent ongoing review of the programme, its results, successes, problems and learning points is crucial. Organisational self-awareness is as important as individual self-awareness from an Authentic Leadership perspective. Just as everything that happens to an individual leader is an opportunity for them to reflect and learn something from a personal/professional perspective, so every organisational initiative, project or collaboration is also an opportunity for the organisation (that is, the *people* in the organisation who make up its management and leadership) to learn something valuable about what works well, what doesn't, and therefore what to do next time to ensure success.

Developing your personal Authentic Leadership

1. Read the 10 Principles of Authentic Leadership in Chapter 8. Which ones resonate with you? Are there any which don't make sense to you at the moment? If there are, these will probably be the most important ones for your own personal leadership journey.

The starting point to developing yourself in any way, either personally or professionally, is always going to be developing your self-awareness, which is the first of the 3 Pillars of Authentic Leadership. This isn't a one-time fix. In fact, it's a focus that you could end up having for the rest of your life! Arguably, developing self-awareness is more an attitude of mind than it is a process. It's an attitude where you are open to experience and are always open to asking yourself self-coaching questions such as: what can I learn from this? What does this mean for me and my relationships with others? What, if anything, could I do differently now and in the future that would be better for myself and others?

If you have completed the exercises in this book you will now know where your preferences and flexibilities are on the People/Task scale, and also on Baron-Cohen's Systemising/Empathising Brain model. This is a good start, as it has implications for many elements of your professional life from how you prefer to learn to the level of detail you are likely to focus on in meetings. There are hundreds of diagnostics available now on the internet, designed to help you to learn something new about yourself, many of them free of charge, and millions of articles which can also prompt your thinking.

2. Be clear about your purpose and outcomes for self-development. It might be to understand yourself better or to become a better manager/leader, or it may be more tangible and focused like getting a promotion or a new job. Be aware though, that if you are engaging with it properly, some of the lessons that you will learn about yourself won't always be comfortable. These are probably some of the most important lessons of all, and your discomfort can become a useful catalyst for change.

3. Write an Action Plan. It needs to be realistic and, ideally, aspirational. The most important thing is that you're committed to it. It may be the kind of action plan where you want to be more or less of something, or it may *be* something more tangible regarding *doing* or *achieving* something.

4. Get yourself a coach and also learn how to self-coach. I often sit down with a blank sheet of paper and ask myself such questions as: What's going on for me right now? What am I happy about/not happy about? If I could change one thing about my working style that would improve my life for the better, what would that be? What am I concerned about? What are my priorities? Is there anything that I have been avoiding and if so do I need to begin to address it now or can it wait a while longer?

You will develop your own set of questions over time that are most useful to you, and you can be flexible with them. It's your time and it's for your benefit. You don't need to share them with anyone. These questions are a way of capturing your thoughts and feelings in a slightly more structured way than Morning Pages for example, which is *stream of consciousness* writing, although you might already use something similar if you write a *Gratitude Diary*.

My personal process is that after I've written everything out so I can see it more clearly on the page, I leave it for a while (sometimes 10 minutes, sometimes a day), and I then re-read it, asking myself if I've missed anything. If I have, I add it. If I haven't, I then destroy the pieces of paper and throw them away, as they've served their purpose. It really helps me to think things through, clarify my priorities and identify anything that I may have unconsciously overlooked.

5. Regularly review your progress against your goals and objectives. Three months is a useful timeframe although you will find what works for you.

You will find more support and suggestions on the book's website *www.unitedbychocolate.com*. If you have a story to tell that you would like to share with others, please post it there.

Epilogue: A New Theory of Leadership

It's my hope that you, and organisations of all kinds will embrace this new theory of leadership with open minds. There's more research to do, and that will come in time. Now at least there is a theory to test and that's a significant contribution to the arena of leadership and leadership development which didn't exist before.

If you would like to complete your own Leadership Temperament Types profile online you will find some questionnaire and report options on the book's website, *www.unitedbychocolate.com*, as well as links, resources, training courses and some more suggestions for your own personal and professional development.

As CEO Mark, one of the case studies said, "The questions you ask are very powerful. I reckon that you're on to something, I really do. It makes complete sense to me."

I hope that it makes complete sense to you too.

I would be delighted if you would contribute your stories, and even your scores, to the book's website. The more examples that we have from real people, and the more examples that we can share of Authentic Leadership in Action, the greater body of evidence that we are going to be able to build around this new theory of leadership, so that for our children, and our children's children, it becomes as familiar and as accepted as equality in the workplace.

If that sounds idealistic, and if also sounds ambitious, I make no apology for it. The world doesn't change for the better by any of us thinking small.

Thank you.

A Note about Her Majesty's Coastguard

You will probably know that Her Majesty's Coastguard operates the Coastal Rescue Service around the 19,000 miles of UK coastline. However, you probably won't be aware that whilst the Coastguard Service is led by uniformed officers who form a part of the Maritime and Coastguard Agency, the 3,500 Coastal Rescue Officers who are ready to be called out on a rescue operation, 24 hours a day, 365 days of the year, including Christmas Day, are all volunteers.

You probably won't be aware either that the Coastal Rescue Service which operates on and around the coast doesn't have any boats! This was a surprise to me too until I learned that the Coastal Rescue Service are trained to operate a search and rescue provision for people in peril in the following terrains:

- mud
- shale, shingle and gravel
- rocks
- sand
- cliffs
- shallow water

If you are unlucky enough to be swept out to sea, or to be in a dangerous situation at sea, once Her Majesty's Coastguard are informed they will involve the other appropriate agencies and co-ordinate your rescue. Out of shallow water, they are most likely to call the UK's most important maritime charity, the Royal National Lifeboat Institution (RNLI) to aid in your rescue, and in very deep water they may even ask the Royal Navy itself for assistance.

For the people who work so hard to keep our beaches and our shores safe, even the loss of one life is one life too many and is a terrible tragedy which they feel very deeply. So please keep safe on the coast and let's hope that you never need to call them.

But if you do, just dial 999 and ask for the Coastguard. They are our 4th Emergency Service.

https://www.gov.uk/government/organisations/maritime-and-coastguard-agency

www.coastguardassociation.com   *www.rnli.org.uk*

Notes and References

These references are really only intended as a starting point for you, if you would like to learn more about any of the ideas, supporting evidence, general subject areas or specific research studies mentioned in the book. What you will find here isn't a comprehensive list by any means, however, it will get you started and setting off in the right direction. There are more resources available on the book's website where you will also find links to those studies and papers mentioned here that already exist as freely available documents.

Chapter One: Gender Stereotypes

1. Fine, C., (2010). *Delusions of Gender.* UK: Icon Books.

2. Baron-Cohen, S., (2003). *The Essential Difference: Men, women and the extreme male brain.* London: Allen-Lane.

3. Larson, F., Lai, M-C., Wagner, A., Baron-Cohen, S., & Holland, A., (2015). *Testing the 'Extreme Female Brain' Theory of Psychosis in Adults with Autism Spectrum Disorder with or without Co-Morbid Psychosis.* PLOS ONE DOI:10.1371/journal.pone.0128102

4. Eagly, A. H. & Steffen, V. J., (1984). Gender stereotypes stem from the distribution of women and men in social roles. *Journal of Personality and Social Psychology*, Vol. 46, (4), pp.735–754.

Chapter Two: Why Women-only Shortlists Don't Work

1. Fine, C., (2010). *Delusions of Gender.* UK: Icon Books.

2. Director Magazine, UK. Women at the Top. July/August 2015, pp.68–73.

   And *https://www.gov.uk/government/publications/women-on-boards-2015-fourth-annual-review* March 2015.

3. Davies Report, 2011

   https://www.gov.uk/government/uploads/system/uploads/attach ment_data/file/31480/11-745-women-on-boards.pdf

4. Women on Boards Davies Review; a Five Year Summary, *https://www.gov.uk/government/publications/women-on-boards-5-year-summary-davies-review* published in October 2015

5. 2015 Cranfield Female FTSE Board Report, *http://www.som.cranfield.ac.uk/som/dinamic-content/research/ftse/FemaleFTSEReportMarch2015.pdf*

6. See reference 1.

7. See reference 1.

8. Koenig, A. M., Eagly, A. H., Mitchell, A. A. & Ristikari, T., (2011). Are Leader Stereotypes Masculine? A Meta-Analysis of Three Research Paradigms. *Psychological Bulletin*, Vol. 137, (4), pp.616–642.

9. Eagly, A. H. & Johannesen-Schmidt, M. C., (2001). The leadership styles of women and men. *Journal of Social Issues*, Vol. 57, (4), pp.781–797

10. Nosek, B. A., Smyth, F. L., Sriram, N., Lindner, N. M., Devos, T., Ayala, A., et al., (2009). National differences in gender-science stereotypes predict national sex differences in science and math achievement. *Proceedings of the National Academy of Sciences*, 106, (26), pp.10593–10597.

11. Eagly, A. H., & Johnson, B. T., (1990). Gender and Leadership Style: A Meta-Analysis. *Psychological Bulletin*, Vol. 108, (2), pp.233–256.

12. See reference 11.

13. Eagly, A. H., Johannesen-Schmidt, M. C., & van Engen, M., L., (2003). Transformational, Transactional and Laissez-Faire Leadership Styles: A Meta-Analysis Comparing Women and Men. *Psychological Bulletin*, Vol. 129, (4), pp.569–591.

14. See reference 13.

15. Ames, D. R., & Flynn, F. J., (2007). What Breaks a Leader: The Curvilinear Relation Between Assertiveness and Leadership. *Journal of Personality and Social Psychology*, Vol. 92, (2), pp.307–324.

16. Kent, T. W., Blair, C. A., Rudd, H. F., & Schuele, U., (2010). Gender Differences and Transformational Leadership Behaviour: Do Both German Men and Women Lead in the Same Way? *International Journal of Leadership Studies*, Vol. 6, (1), pp.52–66.

17. Andersen, J. A., &Hansson, P. H., (2011). At the end of the road? Differences between women and men in leadership behavior. *Leadership and Organization Development Journal*, Vol. 32, (5), pp.428–441.

18. Haslam, S. A., & Ryan, M. K., (2005). The Glass Cliff: Evidence that Women are Over-Represented in Precarious Leadership Positions. *British Journal of Management*, Vol. 16, (2), pp.81–89.

19. Williams, C. L., (1992) The glass escalator: Hidden advantages for men in the 'female' professions. *Social Problems*, Vol. 39, (3), pp.253–266.

20. Rudman, L. A., Moss-Racusin, C. A., Phelan, J. E. & Nauts, S., (2012). Status incongruity and backlash effects: Defending the gender hierarchy motivates prejudice against female leaders. *Journal of Experimental Social Psychology*, Vol. 48, pp.165–179.

21. Heilman, M. E., Wallen, A. S., Fuchs, D. & Tamkins, M. M., (2004). Penalties for Success: Reactions to women who succeed at male gender-typed tasks. *Journal of Applied Psychology*, Vol. 89, (3), pp.416–427.

22. Bowles, H. R., Babcock, L. & Lai, L., (2007). Social incentives for gender differences in the propensity to initiate negotiations: Sometimes it does hurt to ask. *Organizational Behavior and Human Decision Processes*, Vol. 103, pp.84–103.

23. Hersch, J., (2006). Sex discrimination in the labor market. *Foundations and Trends in Microeconomics*, Vol. 2, (4), pp.281–361.

24. Davies, P. G., Spencer, S. J., Quinn, D. M., & Gerdhardstein, R., (2002). Consuming images: How television commercials that elicit stereotype threat can constrain women academically and professionally. *Personality and Social Psychology Bulletin*, Vol. 28, (12), pp.1615–1628.

25. Eagly, A. H. & Karau, S. J., (1991). Gender and the emergence of leaders: A meta-analysis. *Journal of Personality and Social Psychology*, Vol. 60, (5), pp.685–710.

26. Paustian-Underdahl, S. C., Walker, L. S., & Woehr, D. J., (2014). Gender and perceptions of leadership effectiveness: A meta-analysis of contextual moderators. *Journal of Applied Psychology*, Vol. 99, (6), pp.1129–1145.

27. Mohr, T. S., (2014). Why Women Don't Apply for Jobs Unless They're 100% Qualified. *Harvard Business Review*, August 25th online at https://hbr.org/2014/08/why-women-dont-apply-for-jobs-unless-theyre-100-qualified

28. Beddoes-Jones, F., (1999). *Thinking Styles – Relationship Strategies That Work!* BJA Associates, Grantham, UK.

29. Eagly, A. H., (2014). Keynote presentation at the British Psychological Society, Division of Occupational Psychology Conference, Brighton, UK.

30. Archontaki, D., Lewis, G. J., & Bates, T. C., (2013). Genetic Influences on Psychological Well-Being: A Nationally Representative Study. *Journal of Personality*, Vol. 81, (2), pp.221–230.

Chapter Three: The Four Leadership Temperament Types

1. Fisher, H., (2009) *Why Him Why Her?* Oxford, UK: Oneworld Publications

2. Fisher, H. E., Rich, J., Island, H. D., Marchalik, D., Silver, L. and Zava, D., (2010). *Four Primary Temperament Dimensions Poster* at the annual meeting of the American Psychological Association.

3. Robertson, I., (2012). *The Winner Effect: How Power Affects Your Brain.* Bloomsbury, London, UK.

4. Pennebaker et al., (2004). Testosterone as a social inhibitor: Two case studies of the effect of testosterone treatment on language. *Journal of Abnormal Psychology*, Vol. 113, (113), pp.172-175.

5. Bernhardt, P. C., Dabbs, J. M. Jr., Fielden, J. A., & Lutter, C. D., (1998). Testosterone changes during vicarious experiences of winning and losing among fans at sporting events. *Psychological Behaviour*, Vol. 65, (1), pp.59–62.

Chapter Four: How Hormones and Biology interact and the link to Values

1. Fisher, H.E., Rich, J., Island, H.D., Marchalik, D., Silver, L., & Zava, D., (2010). *Four Primary Temperament Dimensions Based on Neurochemistry.* Poster at the Annual Meeting of the American Psychological Association.

2. Fisher, H. E. & J. A. Thomson, Jr., (2007). Lust, Romance, Attachment: Do the side effects of serotonin-enhancing anti-depressants jeopordise romantic love, marriage and fertility? In *Evolutionary Cognitive Neuroscience.* Platek, S. M., Keenan, J. P. & Shackelford, T. K. (Eds.) pp.245–283. Cambridge, MA: MIT Press.

3. Fisher, H.E., Rich, J., Island, H.D., Marchalik, D., Silver, L., & Zava, D., (2010).
    "DO WE HAVE CHEMISTRY?" *Four Primary Temperament Dimensions in the Process of Mate Choice.* Poster at the Annual Meeting of the American Psychological Association.

4. Zuckerman, M., (2005). *Psychobiology of Personality.* New York, NY: Cambridge University Press.

5. Robertson, I. (2012). *The Winner Effect: How Power Affects Your Brain.* Bloomsbury: London, UK.

6. Yan, Z., Karatsoreos, I. N., & McEwan, B. S., (2014). Estrogen protects against the detrimental effects of repeated stress on glutamatergic transition and cognition. *Molecular Psychiatry,* 19, pp.558–598.

7. Cloninger, C. R., Przybeck, T. R., Svrakic, D. M., & Wetzel, R. D., (1994). *The Temperament and Character Inventory, (TCI).* A guide to its development and use. St. Louis, MO: Center for Psychobiology and Personality, Washington University, US.

8. Olson, R., Camp, C., & Fuller, D., (1984). Curiosity and the need for cognition. *Psychological Report,* Vol. 54, (1), pp.71–74.

9. Flaherty, A. W., (2005). Frontotemporal and dopaminegic control of idea generation and creative drive. *Journal of Comparative Neurology,* Vol. 493, (1), pp.147–153.

10. Baron-Cohen, S., Knickmeyer, R. C., & Belmonte, M. K., (2005). Sex differences in the brain: Implications for explaining autism. *Science,* 310, pp.819–823.

11. Baron-Cohen, S., (2002). The extreme male brain theory of autism. *Trends in Cognitive Sciences,* Vol.6, (6) pp.248–254.

12. Baron-Cohen, S., (2003). *The Essential Difference: Men, women and the extreme male brain.* London: Allen-Lane.

13. Yan, Z., Karatsoreos, I. N., & McEwan, B. S., (2014). Estrogen protects against the detrimental effects of repeated stress on glutamatergic transition and cognition. *Molecular Psychiatry,* 19, pp.558–598.

14. Dabbs, J. M., Jr., & Dabbs, M. G., (2000). Heroes, rogues, and lovers: *Testosterone and behaviour.* New York: McGraw Hill.

15. Dabbs, J. M., Jr., Carr, T. S., & Riad, J. K., (1995). Testosterone, crime and misbehaviour among 692 prison inmates. *Personality and Individual Differences,* Vol. 18, (5), pp.627–633.

16. Neave, N., Laing, S., Fink, B. & Manning, J.T., (2003). *Second to fourth digit ratio, testosterone and perceived male dominance.* Proceedings of the Royal Society of London, B, Vol. 270, pp.2167–2172.

17. See reference 16.

18. Guinote, A., (2007). Power affects basic cognition: Increased attentional inhibition and flexibility. *Journal of Experimental Social Psychology*, Vol. 43, (5), pp.685–697.

19. See reference 5.

20. Bernhardt, P. C., Dabbs, J. M. Jr., Fielden, J. A., & Lutter, C. D., (1998). Testosterone changes during vicarious experiences of winning and losing among fans at sporting events. *Physiology & Behaviour*, Vol. 65, (1), pp.59–62.

21. Pennebaker et al., (2004). Testosterone as a social inhibitor: Two case studies of the effect of testosterone treatment on language. *Journal of Abnormal Psychology*, Vol. 113, (113), pp.172–175.

22. Gettler et al., (2011.) *Longitudinal evidence that fatherhood decreases testosterone in human males.* PNAS, Vol.108, (39) pp.16194–16199.
www.pnas.org/content/108/39/16194
And see Berg, S. J., & Wynne-Edwards, K. E., (2001). Changes in testosterone, cortisol and estradiol levels in men becoming fathers. *Mayo Clinic Proceedings*, Vol. 76, (6), pp.582–592.

23. Paustian-Underdahl, S. C., Walker, L. S., & Woehr, D. J., (2014). Gender and perceptions of leadership effectiveness: A meta-analysis of contextual moderators. *Journal of Applied Psychology*, Vol. 99, (6), pp.1129–1145.

24. See reference 1.

25. Wurtman, R.J. et al., (1989). Carbohydrate cravings, mood changes and obesity. *Journal of Clinical Psychiatry*, 49, pp.37–39.

26. See reference 1.

27. Fisher, H., (2009). *Why Him Why Her?* Oxford, UK: Oneworld Publications.

28. See reference 2.

Chapter 6: Leading, Managing, Influencing

1. Archontaki, D., Lewis, G. J., & Bates, T. C., (2013). Genetic Influences on Psychological Well-Being: A Nationally Representative Study. *Journal of Personality*, Vol. 81, (2), pp.221–230.

Chapter Seven: The Dark Side of Leadership

1. Hogan, R. and Hogan, J., (2001). Assessing Leadership: A View from the Dark Side. *International Journal of Selection and Assessment*, Vol. 9, (1-2), pp.40–51.

2. Hogan, R., Hogan, J. and Kaiser, R., (2009). *Management Derailment*. In S. Zedeck, (ed.) American Psychological Association Handbook of Industrial and Organizational Psychology. NY: APA.

3. See reference 2.

Chapter Eight: Authentic Leadership

1. *http://businessjournal.gallup.com/content/113542/what-followers-want-from-leaders.aspx*

2. Gardner, W. L., Cogliser, C. C., Davis, K. M., & Dickens, M. P. (2011) Authentic Leadership: A review of the literature and research agenda. *The Leadership Quarterly*, 22 (6) pp. 1120–1145.

Chapter Ten: The Future of the Boardroom

1. Women on Boards Davies Review; a Five Year Summary, *https://www.gov.uk/government/publications/women-on-boards-5-year-summary-davies-review* published in October 2015

Lightning Source UK Ltd.
Milton Keynes UK
UKOW02f1056131215

264642UK00001B/19/P